Roads – *at scales larger than 1:3 million*
Motorway/Highway
Other Main Road
– *at scales smaller than 1:3 million*
Principal Road: Motorway/Highway
Other Main road
Main Railway

Towns & Cities
☐   Population > 5,000,000
☐   1–5,000,000
○   500,000–1,000,000
○   < 500,000
☐ **Paris**   National Capital
✈   Airport
International Boundary
International Boundary – not defined or in dispute
Internal Boundary
River
Canal
Marsh or Swamp

Relief
▲ 1510   Peak (meters)

5,000 meters (16,405 feet)
4,000 (13,124)
3,000 (9,843)
2,000 (6,562)
1,000 (3,281)
500 (1,641)
200 (656)
100 (328)
0
Land below sea level

Note:
The 0–100 contour layer
appears only at scales
larger than 1:3 million

2

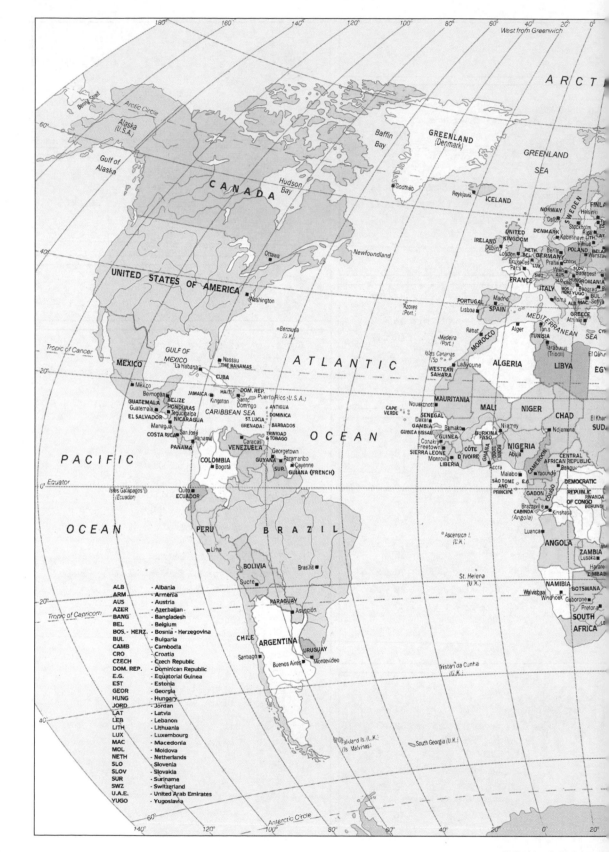

ALB   - Albania
ARM   - Armenia
AUS   - Austria
AZER   - Azerbaijan
BANG   - Bangladesh
BEL   - Belgium
BOS.- HERZ. - Bosnia - Herzegovina
BUL   - Bulgaria
CAMB   - Cambodia
CRO   - Croatia
CZECH   - Czech Republic
DOM. REP. - Dominican Republic
E.G.   - Equatorial Guinea
EST   - Estonia
GEOR   - Georgia
HUNG   - Hungary
JORD   - Jordan
LAT   - Latvia
LEB   - Lebanon
LITH   - Lithuania
LUX   - Luxembourg
MAC   - Macedonia
MOL   - Moldova
NETH   - Netherlands
SLO   - Slovenia
SLOV   - Slovakia
SUR   - Suriname
SWZ   - Switzerland
U.A.E.   - United Arab Emirates
YUGO   - Yugoslavia

Scale 1:85 500 000

3

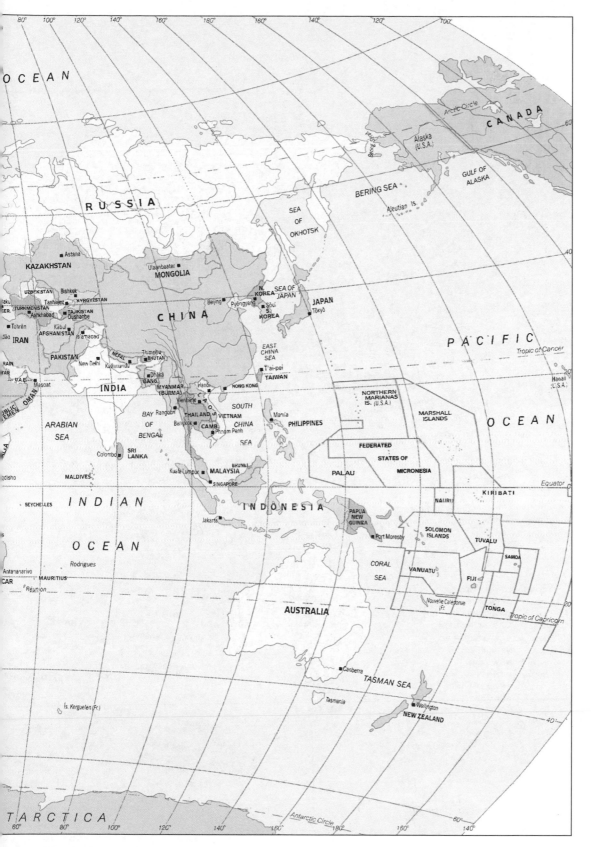

OCEAN

CANADA

Arctic Circle

Alaska
(U.S.A.)

Bering

60

GULF OF
ALASKA

RUSSIA

BERING SEA

40

Aleutian Is.

SEA
OF
OKHOTSK

■ Astana

KAZAKHSTAN

Ulaanbaatar ■

MONGOLIA

SEA OF
JAPAN

N.
KOREA

UZBEKISTAN   Bishkek ■

aku ■

TURKMENISTAN   Tashkent ■   KYRGYZSTAN

ER.

Ashkhabad ■   TAJIKISTAN

Dushanbe ■

CHINA

Beijing ■   Pyŏngyang ■

Sŏul   S.
■ KOREA

JAPAN

Tōkyō ■

PACIFIC

Tropic of Cancer

20

■ Tehrān

Jão

Kābul ■

IRAN   AFGHANISTAN   Islamabad ■

EAST
CHINA
SEA

RAIN

PAKISTAN

NEPAL   Thimphu ■

New Delhi ■   BHUTAN
Kathmandu ■

T'ai-pei ■

TAIWAN

Hawaii
(U.S.A.)

U.A.E.

Masqat ■

INDIA

■ Dhaka
BANG.

MYANMAR
(BURMA)

HONG KONG

NORTHERN
MARIANAS
IS. (U.S.A.)

OCEAN

PUBLIC

EMEN

ARABIAN
SEA

BAY   Rangoon ■
OF   Bangkok ■
BENGAL

THAILAND

Vientiane ■

SOUTH
VIETNAM

CHINA

Hanoi ■

Manila ■

SEA   CAMB.   Phnom Penh ■

PHILIPPINES

MARSHALL
ISLANDS

FEDERATED

OMAN

adisho

■ Colombo   SRI
LANKA

STATES OF

PALAU

MICRONESIA

MALDIVES

Kuala Lumpur ■   MALAYSIA   BRUNEI

Equator

SEYCHELLES

INDIAN

SINGAPORE

INDONESIA

NAURU

KIRIBATI

PAPUA
NEW
GUINEA

SOLOMON
ISLANDS

TUVALU

Jakarta ■

OCEAN

Rodrigues

Antananarivo
CAR   MAURITIUS
Réunion

Port Moresby ■

VANUATU

CORAL
SEA

SAMOA

FIJI

Nouvelle Calédonie
(Fr.)

TONGA

Tropic of Capricorn

20

AUSTRALIA

■ Canberra   TASMAN SEA

Ís. Kerguelen (Fr.)

Tasmania

Wellington ■
NEW ZEALAND

40

TARCTICA

Antarctic Circle

60

4

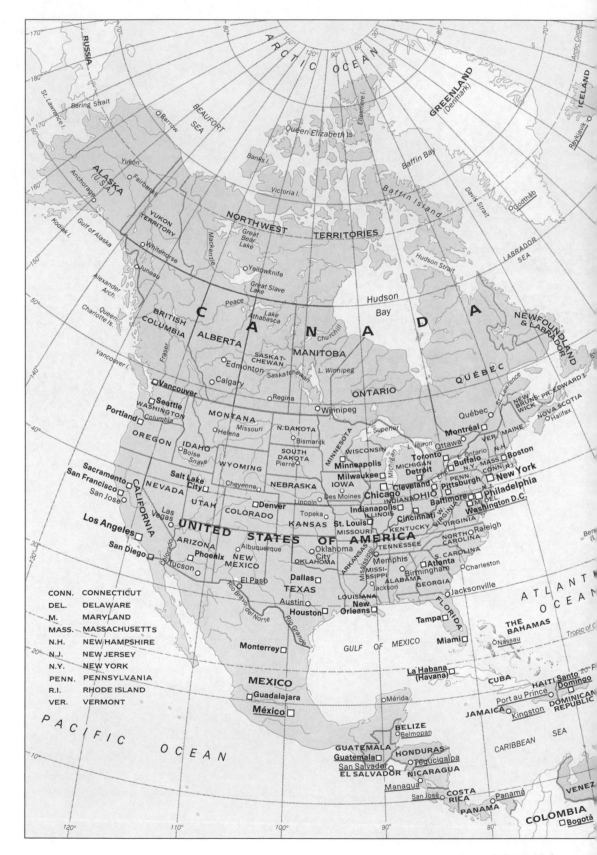

RUSSIA

ARCTIC OCEAN

GREENLAND (Denmark)

ICELAND

Arctic Circle

St. Lawrence I.

Bering Strait

O Barrow

BEAUFORT SEA

Queen Elizabeth Is.

Ellesmere I.

Reykjavik

Kodiak I.

Gulf of Alaska

ALASKA (U.S.A.)

O Fairbanks

Anchorage O

Banks I.

Victoria I.

Baffin Bay

Baffin Island

Godthåb O

YUKON TERRITORY

Great Bear Lake

NORTHWEST TERRITORIES

Hudson Strait

LABRADOR SEA

Whitehorse O

Mackenzie

O Yellowknife

Alexander Arch.

Juneau O

Great Slave Lake

Hudson Bay

NEWFOUNDLAND & LABRADOR

Queen Charlotte Is.

BRITISH COLUMBIA

Peace

ALBERTA

Lake Athabasca

C A N A D A

Fraser

Churchill O

Vancouver I.

SASKAT-CHEWAN

Edmonton O

MANITOBA

L. Winnipeg

Saskatchewan

QUÉBEC

Vancouver □

Calgary O

ONTARIO

Regina O

St. Lawrence

PR. EDWARD I.

Seattle □

WASHINGTON

Winnipeg O

NEW BRUNS-WICK

NOVA SCOTIA

Portland □

Columbia

MONTANA

Missouri

N. DAKOTA

L. Superior

Québec □

MAINE

Halifax O

OREGON

IDAHO

O Helena

Bismarck O

Ottawa

Montréal □

Boise O

SOUTH DAKOTA

MINNESOTA

WISCONSIN

L. Huron

L. Ontario

N.H.

VER.

Boston □

Sacramento □

Snake

WYOMING

Pierre O

Minneapolis □

MICHIGAN

Toronto □

Buffalo □

N.Y.

MASS.

CONN. R.I.

San Francisco □

NEVADA

Salt Lake City □

Milwaukee □

Detroit □

Cleveland □

Erie

Pittsburgh □

PENN.

New York □

San Jose □

CALIFORNIA

UTAH

Cheyenne O

NEBRASKA

IOWA

Chicago □

Des Moines O

ILLINOIS

INDIANA

OHIO

N.J.

Philadelphia □

DEL.

Baltimore □

M.

Washington D.C. □

Las Vegas O

Denver □

COLORADO

Lincoln O

Indianapolis □

Cincinnati □

W. VIRGINIA

VIRGINIA

Los Angeles □

Topeka O

St. Louis □

MISSOURI

KANSAS

KENTUCKY

NORTH CAROLINA

Raleigh O

ARIZONA

Albuquerque O

UNITED STATES OF AMERICA

Oklahoma City O

TENNESSEE

ARKANSAS

Memphis O

S. CAROLINA

San Diego □

Phoenix □

NEW MEXICO

Colorado

O Tucson

OKLAHOMA

Mississippi

Birmingham O

Atlanta □

Charleston O

ALABAMA

GEORGIA

El Paso O

Dallas □

Jackson O

MISSI-SSIPPI

Jacksonville O

Rio Bravo del Norte

TEXAS

LOUISIANA

New Orleans □

FLORIDA

ATLANTIC OCEAN

Austin O

Houston □

Tampa □

Monterrey □

Rio Grande

GULF OF MEXICO

Miami □

THE BAHAMAS

Tropic of C

Nassau O

La Habana (Havana) □

CUBA

HAITI

Santo Domingo □

MEXICO

Guadalajara □

Mérida O

JAMAICA

Port au Prince O

Kingston

DOMINICAN REPUBLIC

México □

P A C I F I C   O C E A N

BELIZE

Belmopan O

GUATEMALA

Guatemala □

HONDURAS

Tegucigalpa O

CARIBBEAN SEA

San Salvador O

NICARAGUA

EL SALVADOR

Managua O

COSTA RICA

San José O

Panamá O

PANAMA

VENEZ

COLOMBIA

Bogotá □

CONN.   CONNECTICUT
DEL.   DELAWARE
M.   MARYLAND
MASS.   MASSACHUSETTS
N.H.   NEW HAMPSHIRE
N.J.   NEW JERSEY
N.Y.   NEW YORK
PENN.   PENNSYLVANIA
R.I.   RHODE ISLAND
VER.   VERMONT

Scale 1:41 600 000

0   500   1000   1500 km

0   250   500   750   1000 miles

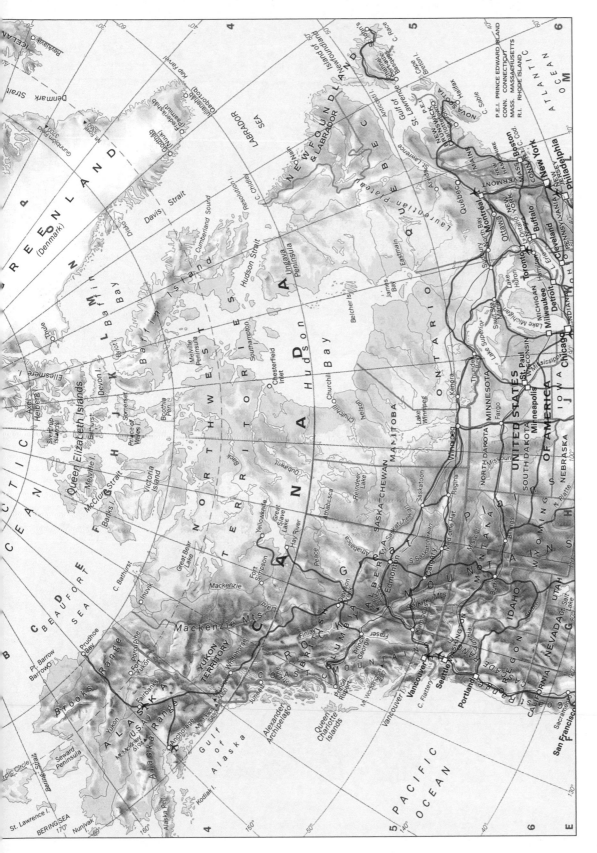

Scale 1:30 000 000

| 0 | 250 | 500 | 750 | 1000 km |

| 0 | 150 | 300 | 450 | 600 miles |

6

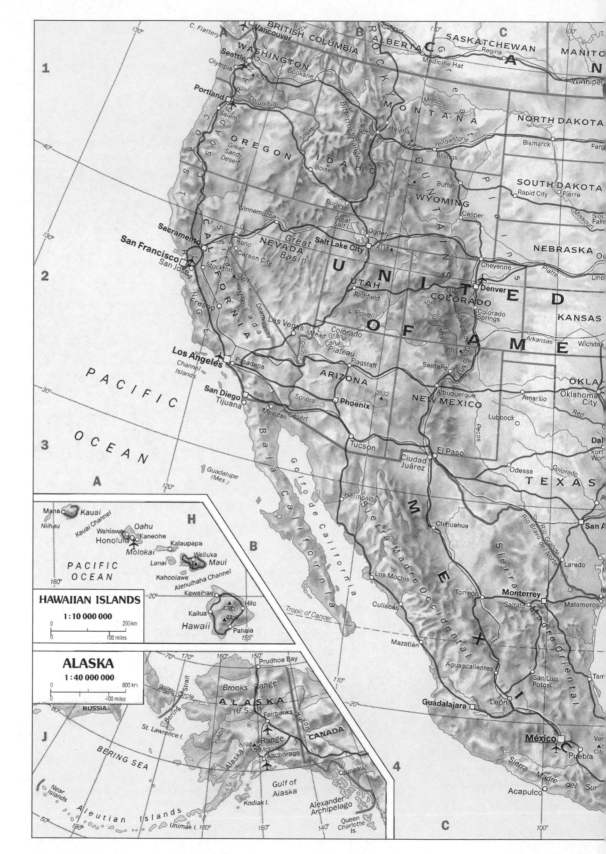

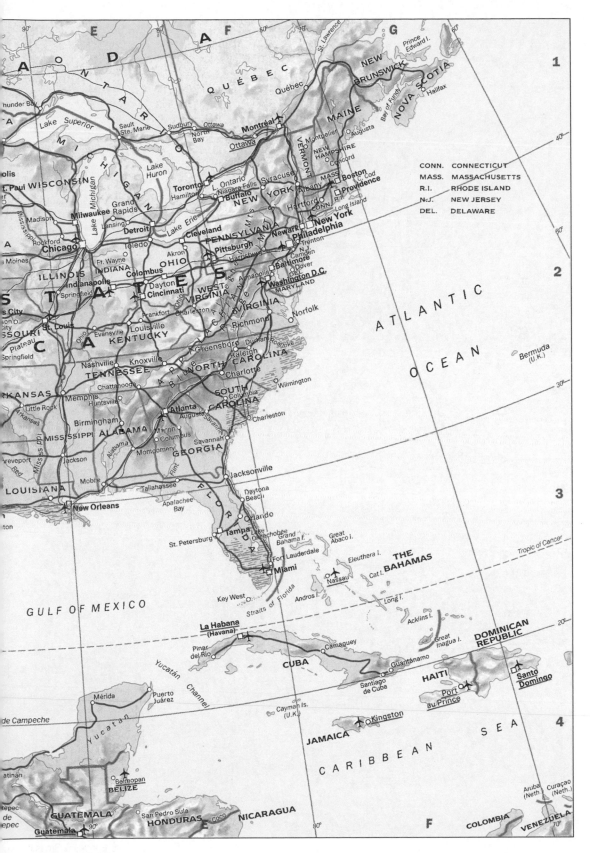

CONN.   CONNECTICUT
MASS.   MASSACHUSETTS
R.I.   RHODE ISLAND
N.J.   NEW JERSEY
DEL.   DELAWARE

8

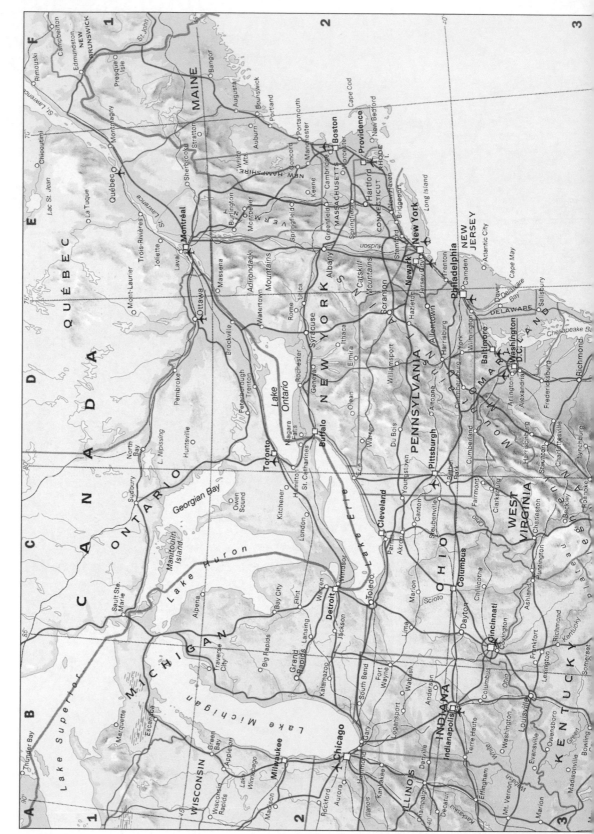

Scale 1:8 600 000

0   100   200   300 km

0   100   200 miles

9

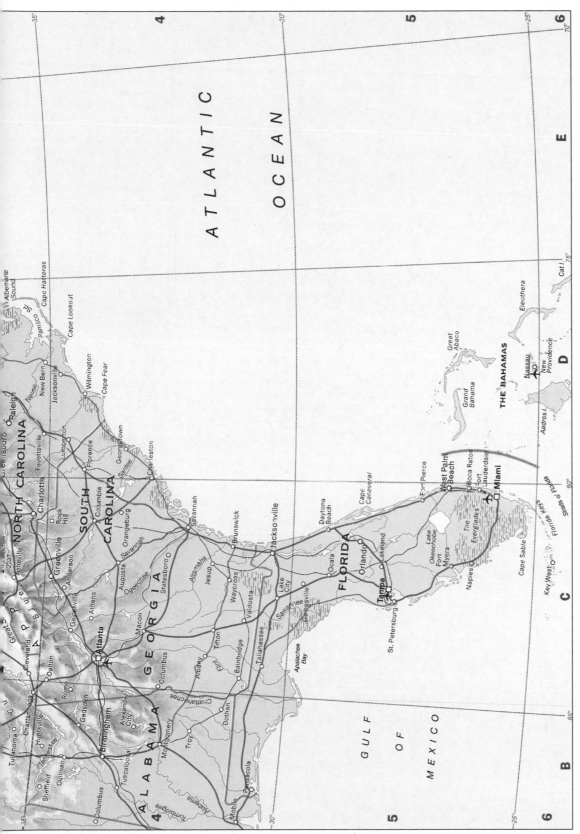

10

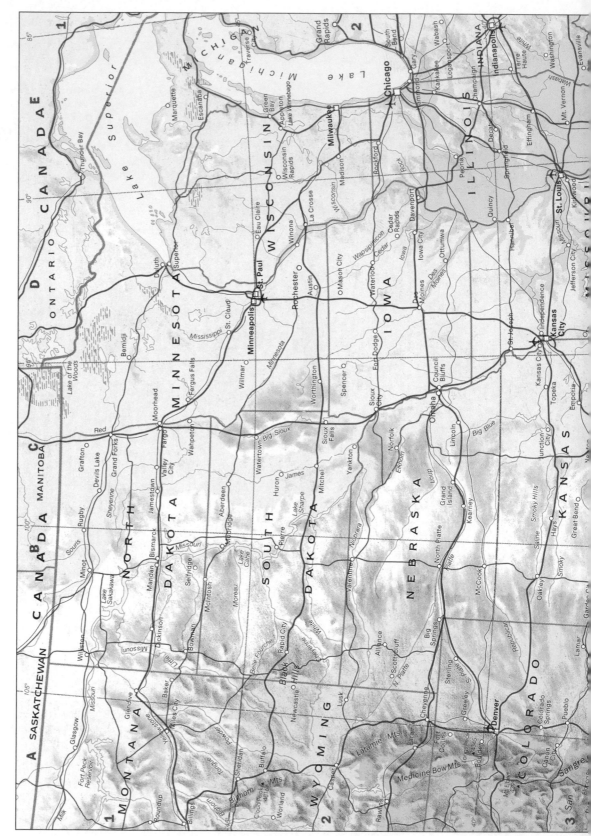

Scale 1:8 600 000

| 0 | 100 | 200 | 300 km |

| 0 | 100 | 200 miles |

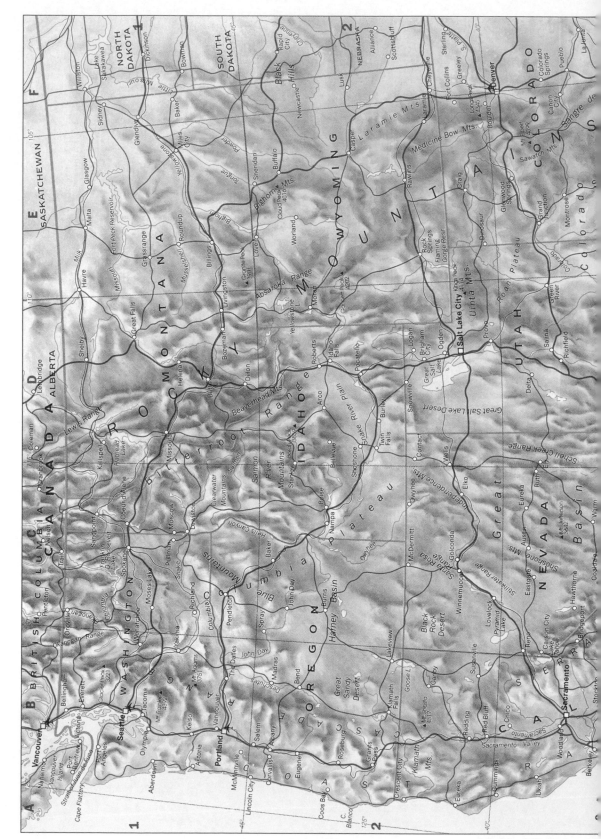

Scale 1:8 600 000

| 0 | 100 | 200 | 300 km |

| 0 | 100 | 200 miles |

13

14

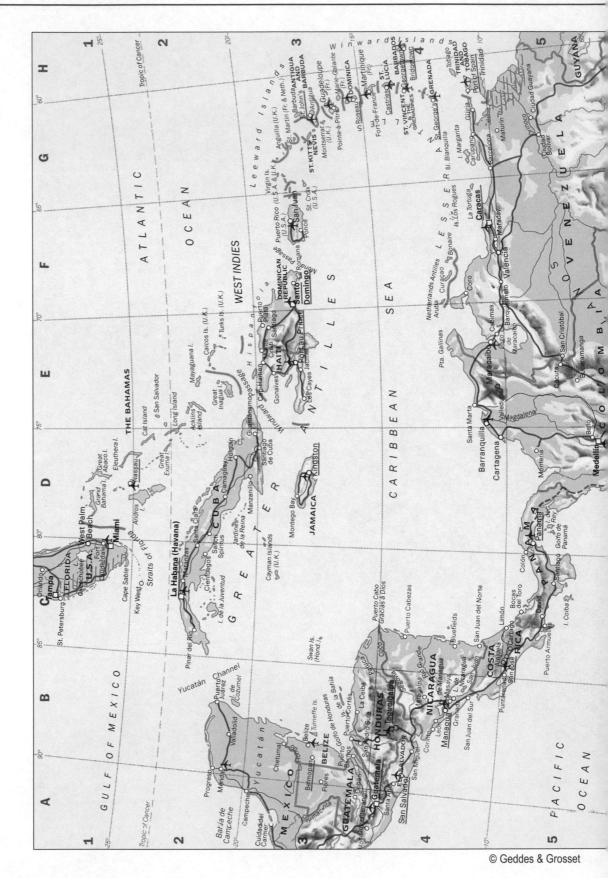

Scale 1:17 000 000

| 0 | 200 | 400 | 600 | 800 km |

| 0 | 250 | | 500 miles |

NORTH

ATLANTIC

OCEAN

Martinique (Fr.)
ST. LUCIA
ST. VINCENT
& THE GRENADINES
BARBADOS
GRENADA
Netherlands
Antilles
Curaçao
Barranquilla
Maracaibo
Güiria
TRINIDAD AND TOBAGO
Caracas
Panamá
Cartagena
Barquisimeto
Barcelona
Port of Spain
PANAMA
Monteria
L. Maracaibo
Rinoco
Ciudad Guayana
VENEZUELA
Georgetown
Medellín
Paramaribo
Cayenne
Bogotá
GUYANA
SURINAME
GUIANA
(FRENCH)
Cali
COLOMBIA
Boa Vista
Macapá
Eguator
Quito
ECUADOR
Negro
Amazonas
Belém
São
Luis
Parnaiba
Guayaquil
Manaus
Santarém
Fortaleza
Loja
Iquitos
Amazonas
Teresina
Imperatriz
Natal
Trujillo
Cruzeiro do
Sul
Lábrea
Humaitá
Madeira
Carolina
Recife
PERU
Rio Branco
Pôrto Velho
Juàzeiro
Maceió
Ucayali
Madre de Dios
Xingu
São Francisco
Lima
Callao
Huancayo
Cuzco
Salvador
L. Titicaca
Cuiabá
Brasília
Arequipa
La Paz
BOLIVIA
Goiânia
Oruro
Santa
Cruz
Arica
Sucre
Corumbá
Belo
Horizonte
Campo
Grande
Vitória
Antofagasta
PARAGUAY
Campinas
of Capricorn
Concepción
Paraná
Rio de Janeiro
Salta
Asunción
São Paulo
Tropic of Capricorn
San Miguel
de Tucumán
Foz do
Iguacú
Curitiba
PACIFIC
Florianópolis
Uruguay
San Juan
Córdoba
Santa
Fé
Concordia
Pôrto Alegre
SOUTH
Viña del Mar
Paraná
Salto
Rio Grande
Santiago
Rosario
Mendoza
URUGUAY
ATLANTIC
OCEAN
Montevideo
Buenos Aires
ARGENTINA
Concepción
Mar del Plata
OCEAN
Bahía Blanca
Neuquén
Puerto Montt
Comodoro
Rivadavia
Falkland Is.
(Is. Malvinas)
(U.K.)
Rio Gallegos
Stanley
Est. de
Magallanes
Tierra del
Fuego
Punta Arenas
South Georgia
(U.K.)

Scale 1:37 000 000

| 0 | 400 | 800 | 1200 | 1600 km |

| 0 | 200 | 400 | 600 | 800 | 1000 miles |

16

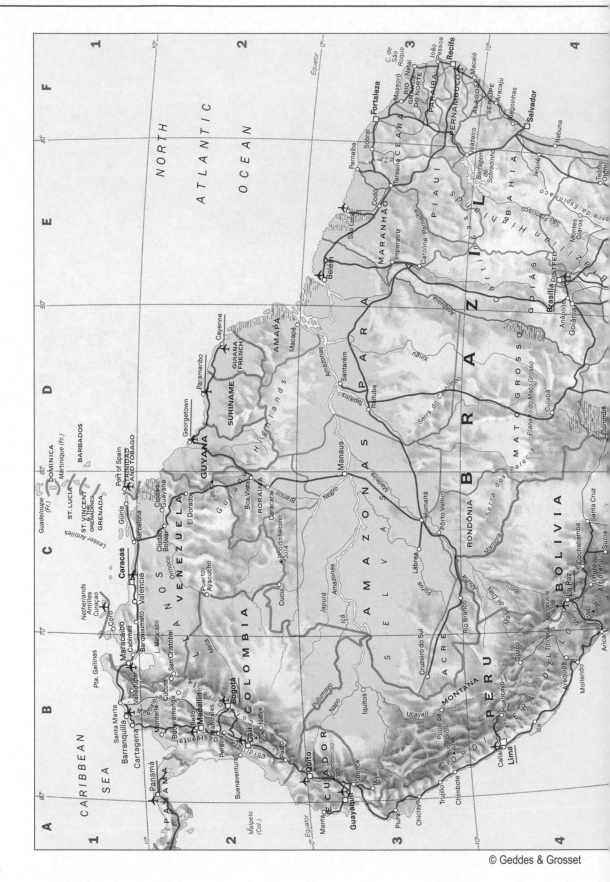

Scale 1:25 500 000

| 0 | 200 | 400 | 600 | 800 | 1000 km |

| 0 | 150 | 300 | 450 | 600 miles |

17

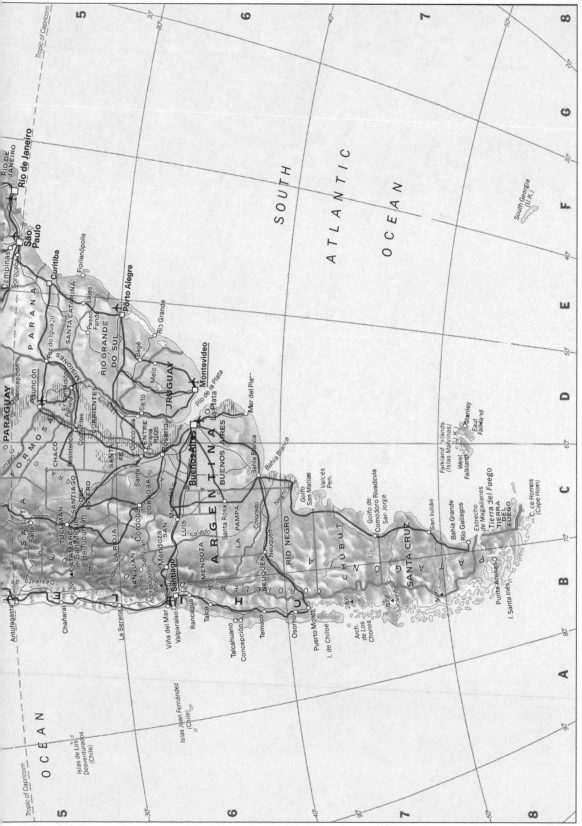

18

© Geddes & Grosset

Scale 1:25 500 000

0   200   400   600   800   1000 km

0   150   300   450   600 miles

Scale 1:8 000 000

| 0 | 100 | 200 | 300 km |

| 0 | 100 | 200 mile |

20

Scale 1:2 600 000

| 0 | 20 | 40 | 60 | 80 | 100 km |

| 0 | 15 | 30 | 45 | 60 miles |

21

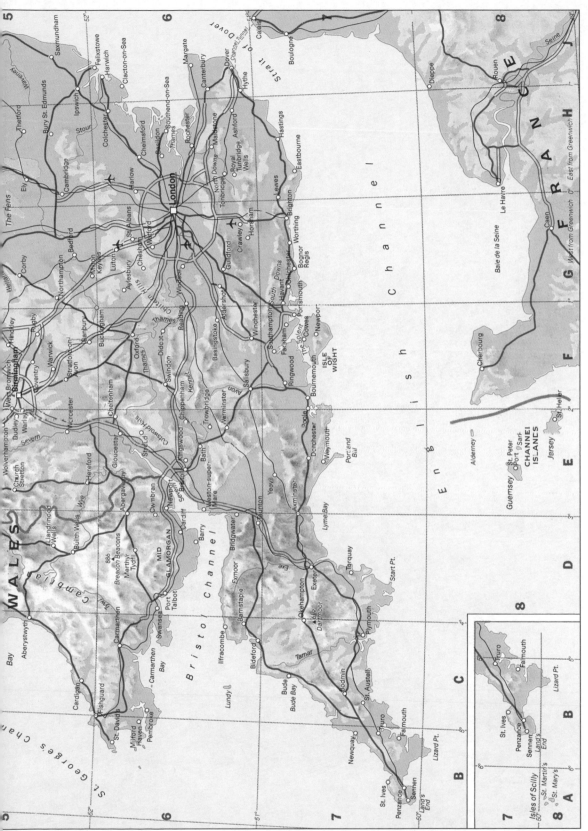

22

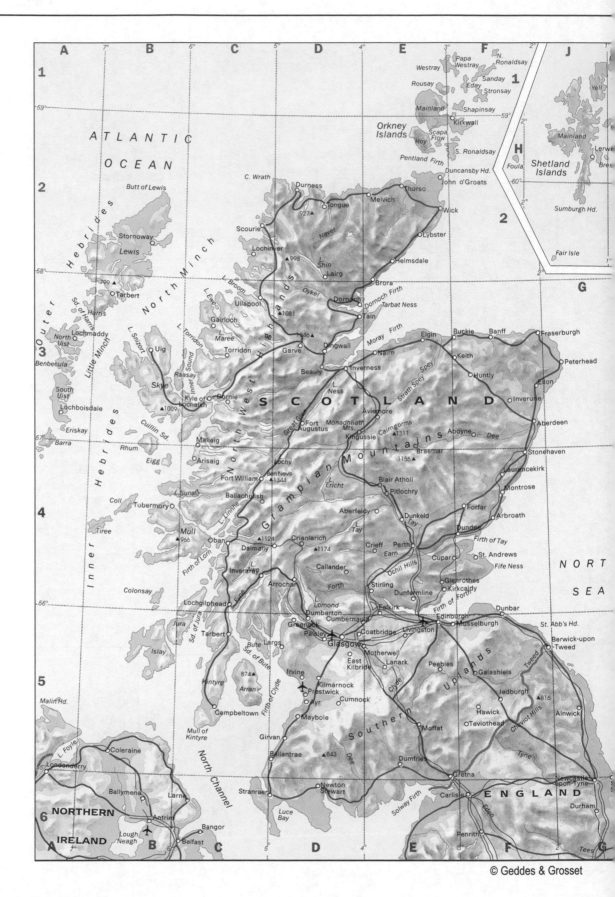

Scale 1:2 600 000

0   20   40   60   80   100 km

0   15   30   45   60 miles

A 10° B 9° C 8° D 7° E 6° F G

SCOTLAND

Greenock
56°
Tarbert
Jura
Islay
Arran
1
Ayr
Cambeltown

Malin Hd.
Inishowen Pen.
▲615
Rathlin I.
Fair Hd.
North Channel
Falcarragh
L. Swilly
Portrush
752 ▲
Letterkenny
L. Foyle
Coleraine
Stranraer
55°
Aran I.
Foyle
Londonderry
Bann
Ballymena
554 ▲
Mts. of Antrim
Larne
Derryveagh Mts.
Finn
Strabane
Dungiven
Ardara
Sperrin ▲ Mts.
676 ▲
683
Newtown-
Rossan Pt.
abbey
Belfast L.
NORTHERN
Antrim
Donegal
Lough
Bangor
Donegal
Omagh
IRELAND
Neagh
Belfast
2
Bay
Lisburn
Strangford L.
Bundoran
Ballygawley
Lurgan
Lagan
Lower
Erris Hd.
Lough Erne
Armagh
Dundrum
Belmullet
Enniskillen
Bann
380 ▲
Sligo Bay
Upper
Monaghan
852 ▲
Dundrum
Blacksod
Killala Bay
Lough
Newry
Mourne
Bay
Sligo
Belcoo
Erne
Mts.
Bay
Ballina
Collooney
Dundalk
Isle of
Achill I.
807 ▲
Moy
Carrickmacross
Man
L. Conn
Boyle
Carrick on
Cavan
Dundalk
54°
Clare I.
Shannon
Bay
Castlebar
Dunleer
IRISH
Clew
Westport
Bay
Longford
Kells
Drogheda
Claremorris
Edgeworthstown
An Uaimh
Boyne
Killary
Roscommon
(Navan)
Balbriggan
Harbour
L. Mask
Lough
3
Clifden
Ree
Mullingar
SEA
L. Corrib
Athlone
Slyne Hd.
Kinnegad
Howth Hd.
Ballinasloe
Dublin
Galway
Brosna
Liffey
Bay
Athenry
Tullamore
Dublin
Kilkieran Bay
Suck
Cloghan
Bog of Allen
Dun Laoghaire
Galway Bay
Kinvarra
Birr
Naas
Bray
Aran Is.
Gort
Shannon
Port
850 ▲
Laoise
Wicklow
Hags Hd.
Derg
Roscrea
526 ▲
Wicklow
53°
Ennistymon
IRELAND
Barrow
Wicklow Hd.
Ennis
Nenagh
Durrow
Carlow
Arklow
▲695
Slaney
Kilrush
Thurles
Kilkenny
Loop Hd.
Limerick
Golden Vale
Enniscorthy
4
Tarbert
Tipperary
Cashel
Wexford
Shannon
▲722
New Ross
Bay
Estuary
Caher
Ráth Luirc
Clonmel
Wexford
Tralee
Feale
Suir
Rosslare
Bay
Knockmealdown
Waterford
Pt.
▲953
Mts.
Carnsore Pt.
Dingle
Mallow
Fermoy
Blackwater
Dungarvan
Fishguard
52°
Dingle Bay
Carrauntoohil
Youghal
▲1041
Killarney
Waterford Harbour
WALES
774 ▲
MacGillicuddy's Reeks
Boggerah Mts
Cork
Kenmare
Cobh
Caha Mts.
Bandon
Cork Harbour
Bantry
Old Head
5
sey Hd.
Bantry Bay
of Kinsale
Mizen Hd.

St. George's Channel

ATLANTIC OCEAN

10° B 9° C 8° D 7° E 6° F 5°

Scale 1:2 600 000

0 20 40 60 80 100 km

0 15 30 45 60 miles

24

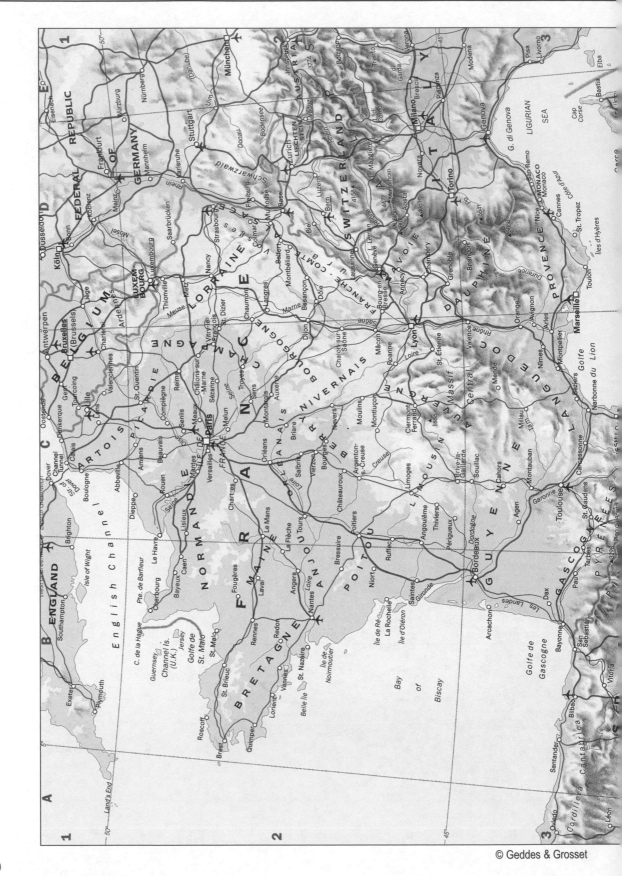

Scale 1:6 500 000

| 0 | 100 | 200 | 300 km |

| 0 | 100 | 200 miles |

25

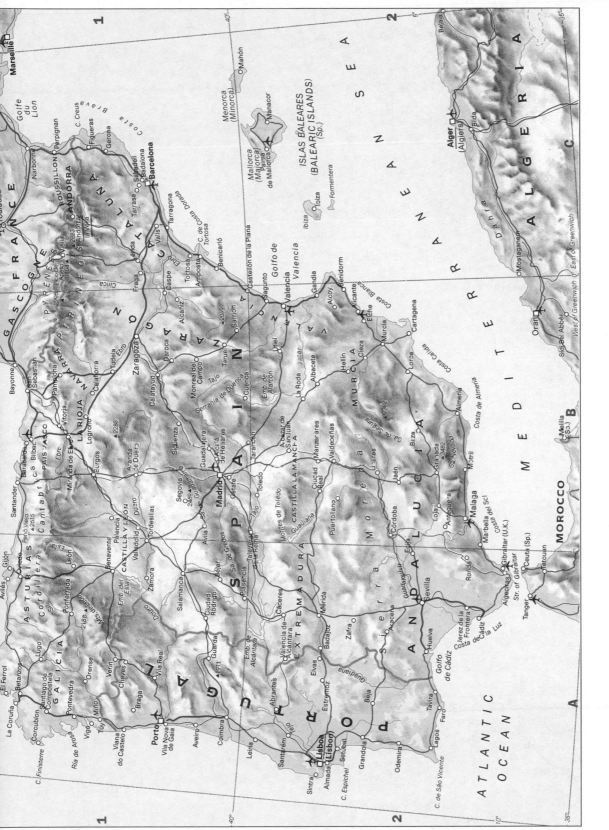

Scale 1:6 500 000

| 0 | 100 | 200 | 300 km |

| 0 | 100 | 200 miles |

© Geddes & Grosset

Scale 1:6 500 000

0   100   200   300 km

0   100   200 miles

28

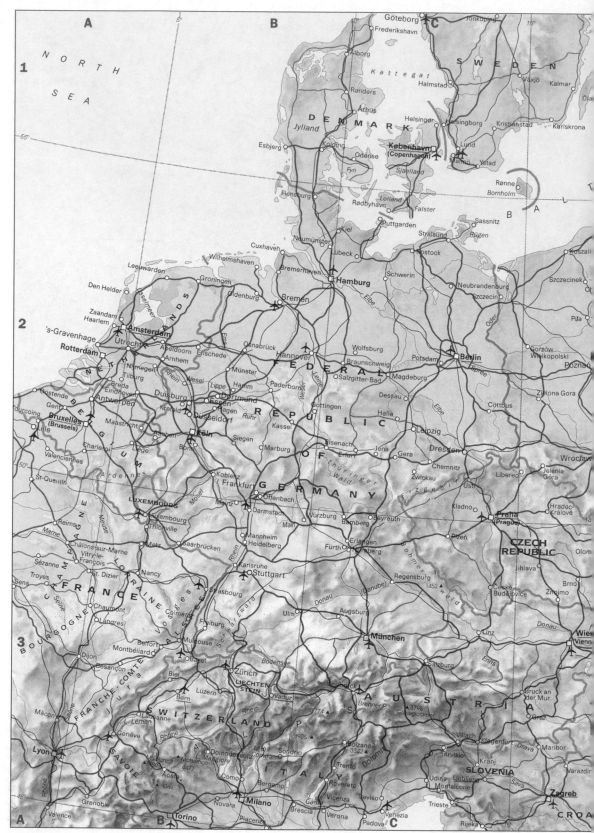

Scale 1:6 500 000

```
0        100       200       300 km
0              100           200 miles
```

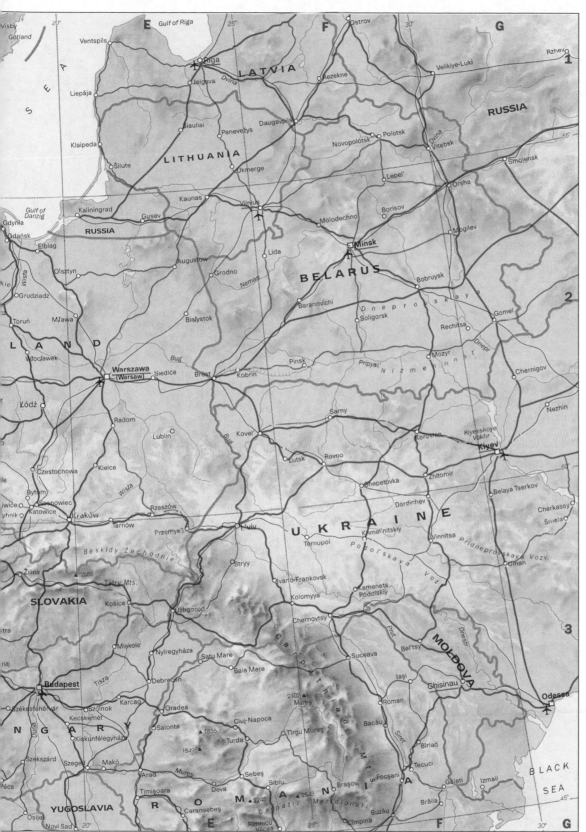

30

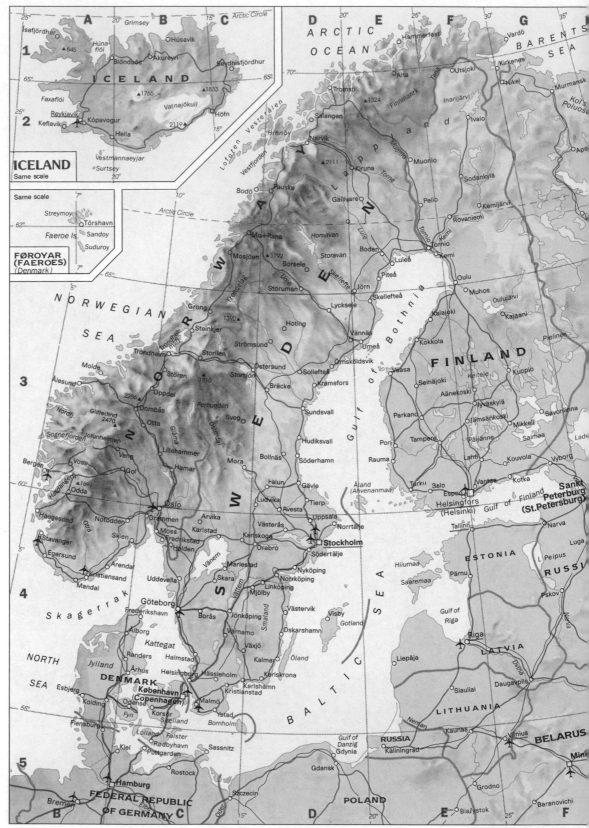

ICELAND
Same scale

Same scale

FØROYAR
(FAEROES)
(Denmark)

Scale 1:9 600 000

0   100   200   300 km

0   100   200 miles

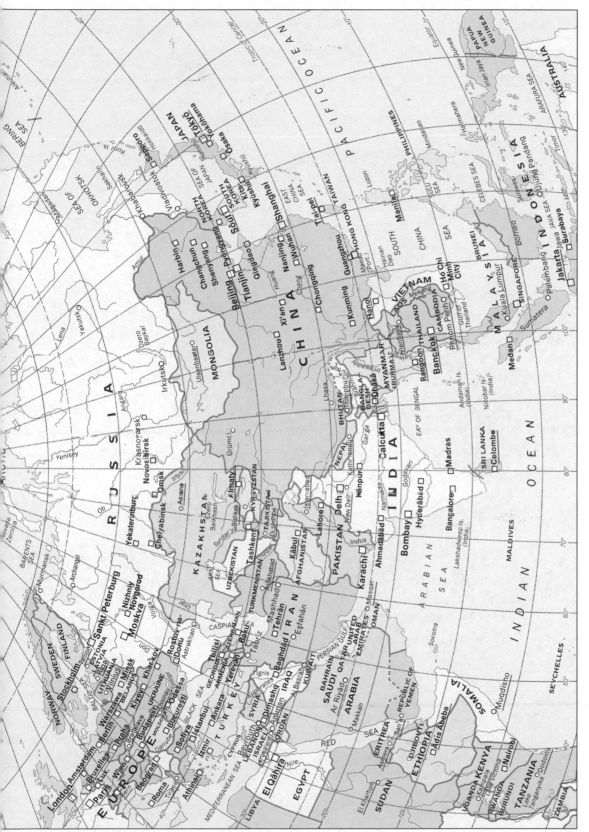

© Geddes & Grosset

Scale 1:60 900 000

0   400   800   1200   1600 km

0   200   400   600   800 1000 miles

32

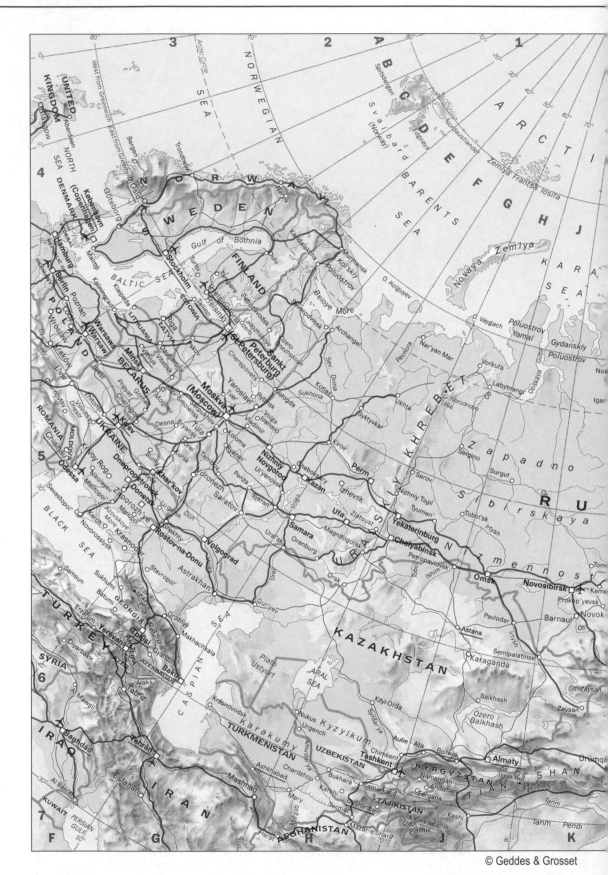

Scale 1:27 000 000

0   200   400   600   800   1000 km

0   150   300   450   600 miles

34

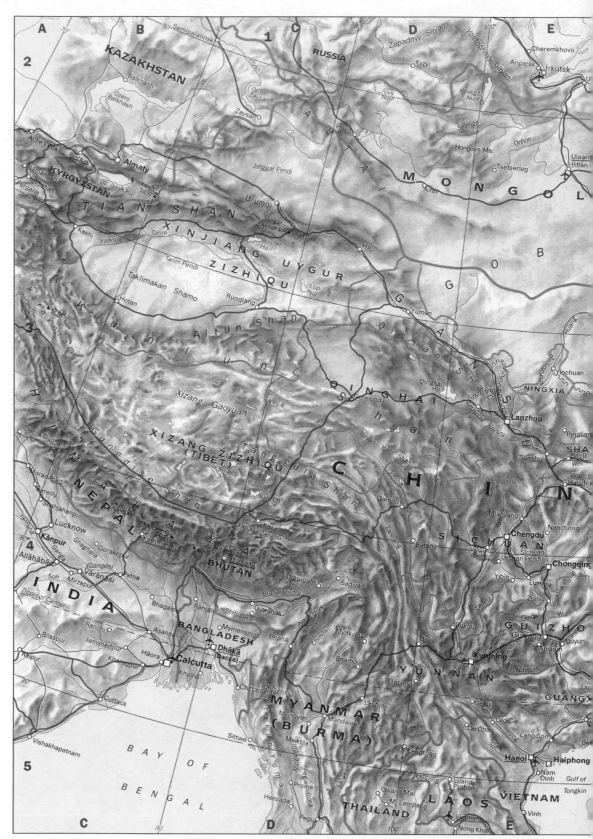

Scale 1:19 500 000

| 0 | 200 | 400 | 600 | 800 km |

| 0 | 100 | 200 | 300 | 400 | 500 miles |

© Geddes & Grosset

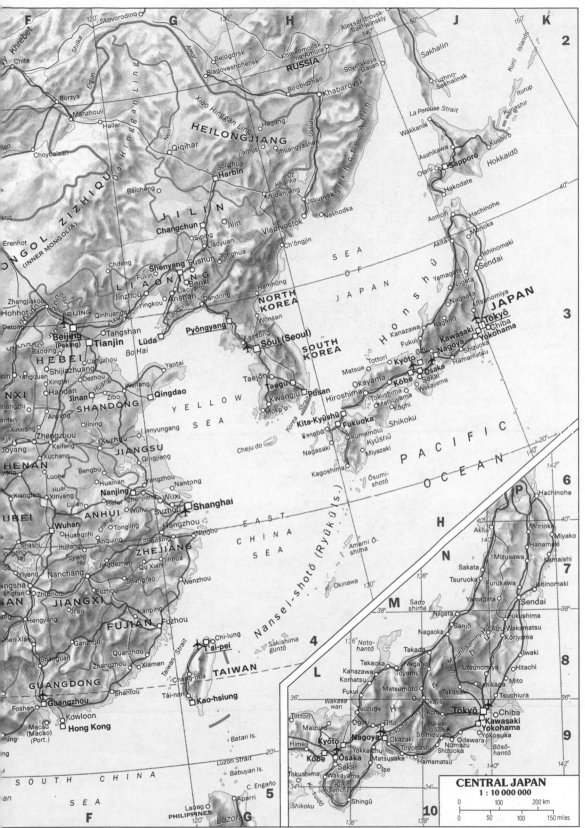

36

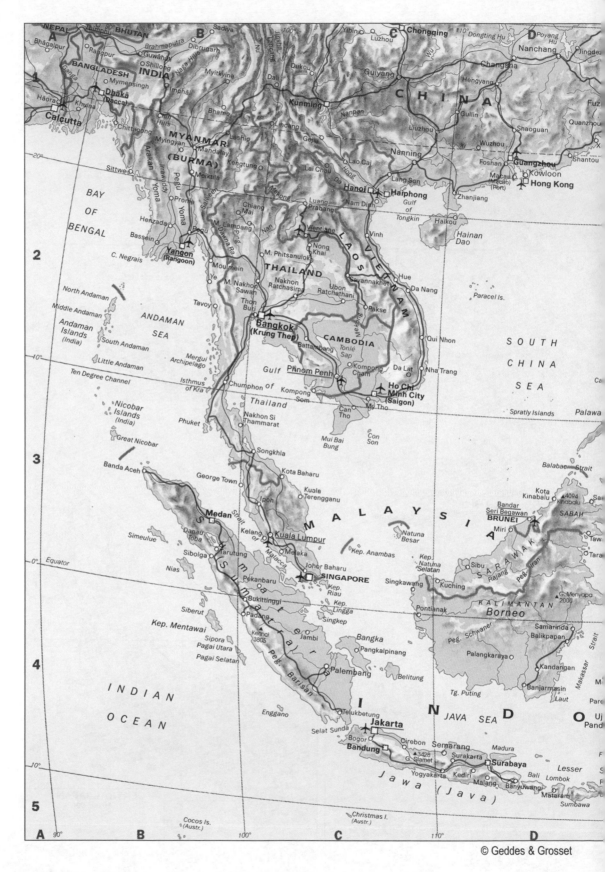

Scale 1:21 000 000

0   200   400   600   800 km

0   100   200   300   400   500 miles

© Geddes & Grosset

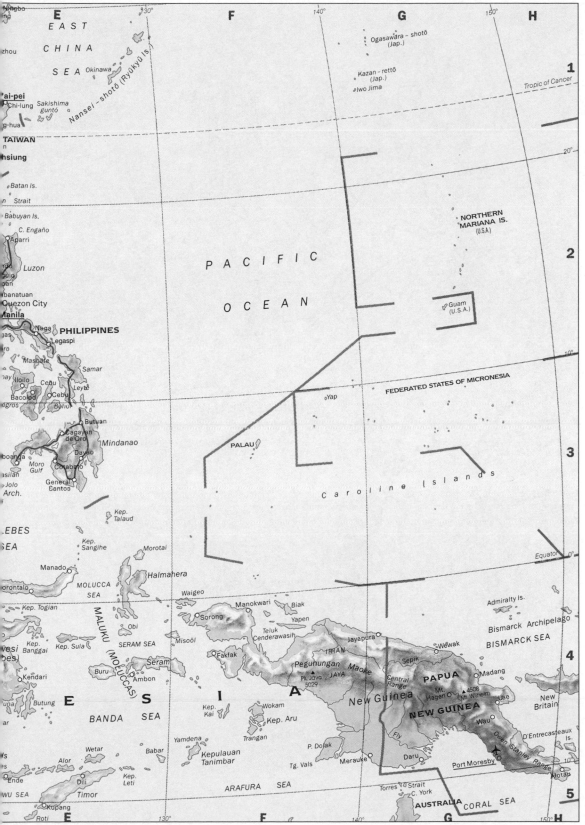

E F G H

Ningbo

EAST

zhou

CHINA

ai-pei   *SEA*   Okinawa

Chi-lung   Sakishima

g-hua   guntó

TAIWAN

n

hsiung

Batan Is.

n   Strait

Babuyan Is.

C. Engaño

Aparri

uio   Luzon

an

banatuan

Quezon City

Manila

Naga   **PHILIPPINES**

as   Legaspi

Masbate

ay   Iloilo   Cebu

Bacolod   Cebu   Leyte

gros   Bohol

boanga   Butuan

Cagayan

de Oro   *Mindanao*

Dayao

basilan   Cotabato

Jolo   General

Arch.   Santos

LEBES

SEA

Kep.

Talaud

Manado

orontalo   MOLUCCA

SEA   Halmahera

Kep. Togian   Waigeo

MALUKU   Sorong   Manokwari   Biak

esi   Obi   Yapen

Kep.   Misoöl   Teluk

Banggai   Kep. Sula   SERAM SEA   Cenderawasih

es)   Seram   IRIAN

Kendari   Buru   Ambon

Butung   E   N   Fakfak   Pegunungan Maoke   JAYA

pa   BANDA   SEA   Pt. Java

5029   New Guinea

ar   Kep.   Wokam

Kai

Kep. Aru   Fly

Yamdena   Trangan

Alor   Wetar   Babar   P. Dolak

Ende   Kepulauan   Tg. Vals   Merauke   Daru

Dili   Kep.   Tanimbar

WU SEA   Leti

Kupang   Timor   ARAFURA   SEA

Roti   E   F

PACIFIC

OCEAN

Ogasawara – shotō

(Jap.)

Kazan – rettō

(Jap.)

Iwo Jima

Tropic of Cancer

20°

NORTHERN

MARIANA IS.

(U.S.A.)

Guam

(U.S.A.)

10°

FEDERATED STATES OF MICRONESIA

Yap

PALAU

C a r o l i n e   I s l a n d s

Equator   0°

Admiralty Is.

Bismarck   Archipelago

BISMARCK SEA

Jayapura   Sepik   Wewak

Central   **PAPUA**   Madang

Range

Mt.   **NEW GUINEA**   New

Hagen   Mt. Wilhelm   Lae   Britain

4508

Wau   D'Entrecasteaux

Is.

Owen Stanley Range   10°

Port Moresby   Motata

Torres   Strait   5

C. York

AUSTRALIA   CORAL   SEA

G   H

1

2

3

4

5

38

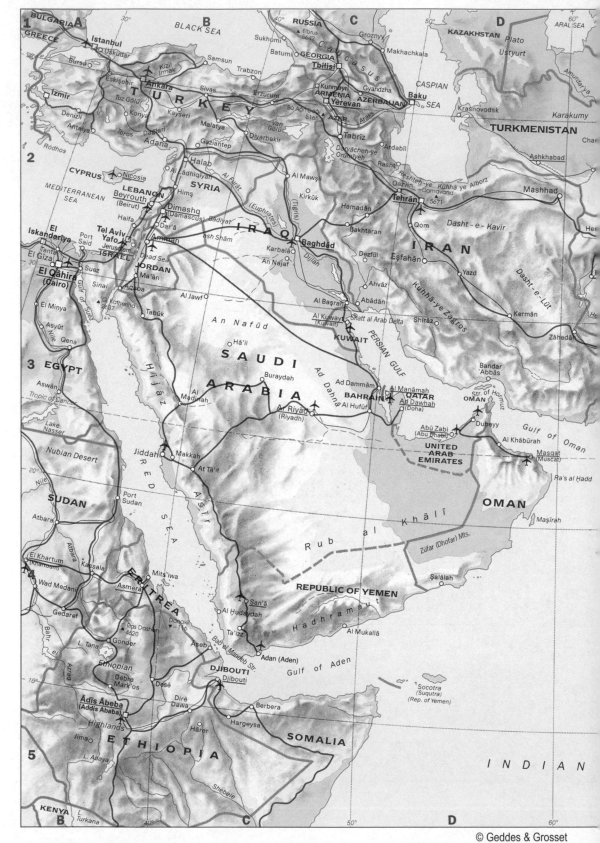

Scale 1:21 000 000

| 0 | 200 | 400 | 600 | 800 km |

| 0 | 100 | 200 | 300 | 400 | 500 miles |

© Geddes & Grosset

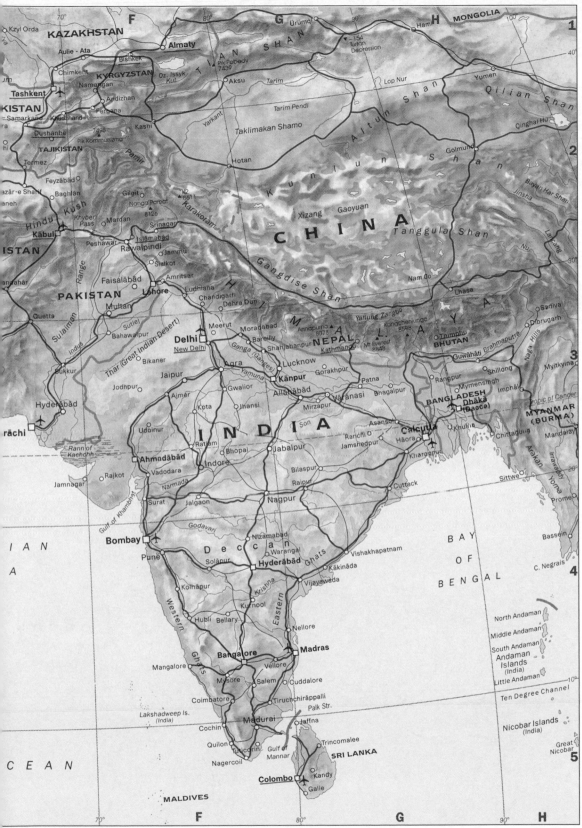

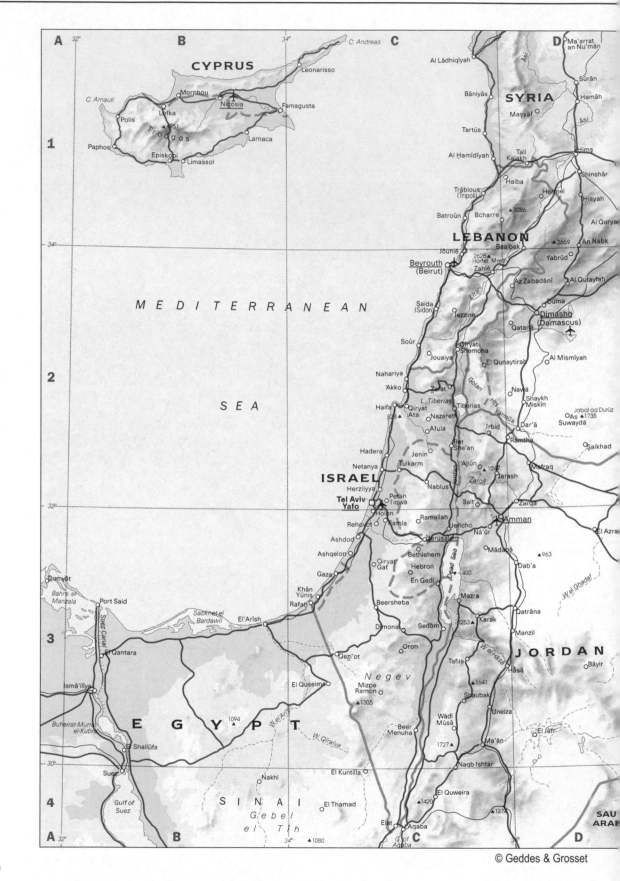

CYPRUS

C. Arnauti

Polis
Paphos
Episkopi
Limassol
Lefka
Troodos
Morphou
Nicosia
Famagusta
Larnaca
Leonarisso
C. Andreas

Al Lādhiqīyah
SYRIA
Maşyāf
Bāniyās
Tartūs
Al Hamīdīyah
Tall Kalakh
Ḥalba
Trâblous (Tripoli)
Batroûn
Bcharre
▲3086
▲2659
An Nabk
Jôunié
Baalbek
LEBANON
Yabrūd
Beyrouth (Beirut)
Hâret Mreff
Zahlê
2628▲
Suḥān
Hamāh
Shinshār
Ḥisyah
Al Qarya
Al Azra
Ma'arrat an Nu'mān
Ḥimş
Az Zabadānī
Al Qutayfah
Dûma
Dimasha (Damascus)
Saïda (Sidon)
Jezzîne
Qatana
Soûr
Jouaiya
Qiryat Shemona
El Qunaytirah
Al Mismīyah
Nahariya
'Akko
Zefat
Golan
Navia
Shaykh Miskin
Jabal od Durūz
Haifa
Qiryat Ata
L. Tiberias
Tiberias
▲1735
Suwaydā
Nazareth
Hts. Yarmūk
Dar'a
As
Afula
Irbid
Bet She'an
Hadera
Jenin
'Ajlūn
Ramtha
Salkhad
Netanya
Tulkarm
Zarqā
1247▲
Mafraq
Jarash
ISRAEL
Nablus
Herzliyya
Petah Tiqwa
Salt
Zarqa
Tel Aviv Yafo
Holon
Ramallah
Jericho
Nâ'ûr
Amman
El Azraq
Rehovot
Ramla
Jerusalem
Mādabā
Ashdod
Bethlehem
Dab'a
Ashqelon
Qiryat Gat
Hebron
▲963
Gaza
En Gedi
▼400
Khān Yūnis
Mazra
W. el Ghadaf
Rafah
Beersheba
Qatrāna
Dumyāt
Bahra el Manzala
Port Said
Sedom
▲1253
Karak
Manzil
Sabkhet el Bardawil
El'Arîsh
Dimona
Oron
Tafila
▲1641
Hâsā
Bâyir
El Qantara
Qezi'ot
JORDAN
Ismâ'iliya
Buheirat-Murrat el-Kubra
El Quseima
N e g e v
Mizpe Ramon
▲1305
Shaubak
Uneiza
El Shallûfa
1094▲
W. el Arîsh
Beer Menuha
Wādī Mûsā
El Jafr
Suez
W. Qiraiya
1727▲
Ma'ân
Nakhl
El Kuntilla
Naqb Ishtar
Gulf of Suez
S I N A I
Gebel el Tîh
El Thamad
El Quweira
El Quweira
▲1420
127▲
Eilat
Aqaba
Gulf of Aqaba
▲1080
SAU... ARA...

M E D I T E R R A N E A N

S E A

E G Y P T

© Geddes & Grosset

Scale 1:3 250 000

0   25   50   75   100 km

0   15   30   45   60 miles

41

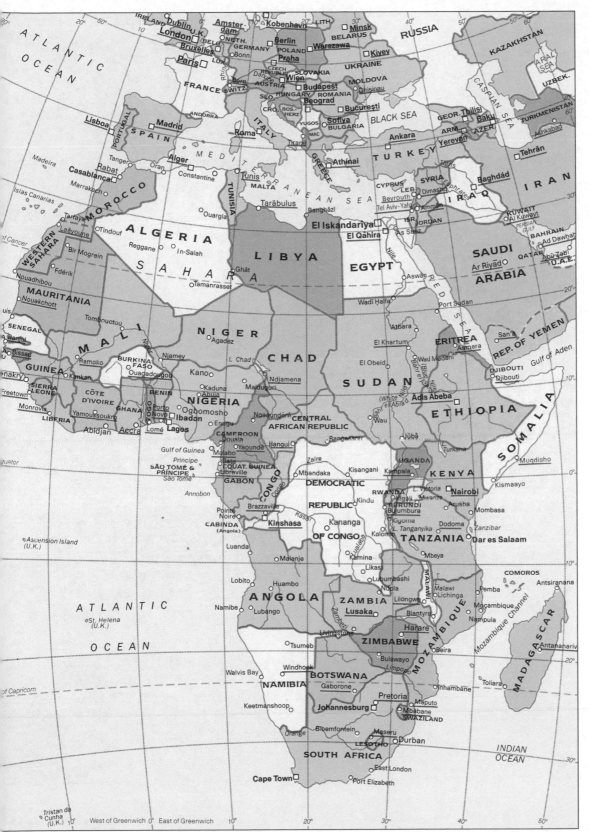

ATLANTIC OCEAN

IRELAND
Dublin
London U.K.
Amsterdam
NETH.
BELG.
Bruxelles
GERMANY
LUX.
Paris
FRANCE
SWITZ.
Bern
Rhine
Kobenhavn
DENMARK
Berlin
Bonn
POLAND
Warszawa
CZECH REPUBLIC
Praha
Wien
AUSTRIA
SLOVAKIA
SLO.
HUNGARY
Budapest
CRO.
BOS.
HERZ.
YUGOS.
MAC.
Danube
Minsk
BELARUS
Kivev
UKRAINE
MOLDOVA
Chisinau
ROMANIA
Bucureşti
Beograd
Sofiya
BULGARIA
Tirane
RUSSIA

KAZAKHSTAN
ARAL SEA
UZBEK.

Lisboa
PORTUGAL
Madrid
SPAIN
ANDORRA
Roma
ITALY
BLACK SEA
GREECE
Athinai
TURKEY
Ankara
GEOR. Tbilisi
ARM.
Yerevan
AZER.
Baku
CASPIAN SEA
TURKMENISTAN
Ashkabad

Madeira
Tanger
Oran
Alger
MEDITERRANEAN SEA
TUNIS
MALTA
Tarābulus
Benghâzi
CYPRUS
LEB.
Beyrouth
Tel Aviv-Yafo
SYRIA
Dimashq
Euphrates
Amman
JORDAN
ISR.
Baghdád
IRAQ
Tigris
IRAN
Tehrān

Casablanca
Rabat
MOROCCO
Constantine
TUNISIA

Islas Canarias
Tarfaya
Laâyoune
Tindouf
WESTERN SAHARA
Bir Mogrein
Fdérik
ALGERIA
Reggane
In-Salah
SAHARA
Ghāt
Tamanrasset
LIBYA
El Iskandarîya
El Qâhira
As Suez
EGYPT
Aswân
RED SEA
SAUDI ARABIA
Ar Riyād
KUWAIT
Al Kuwayt
PERSIAN GULF
BAHRAIN
Ad Dawhah
QATAR
Abū Zabī
U.A.E.

of Cancer

Nouadhibou
Nouakchott
MAURITANIA
SENEGAL
Tombouctou
Bamako
MALI
Niger
NIGER
Agadez
CHAD
L. Chad
Njamey
Kano
Ndjamena
Maiduguri
Kaduna
BURKINA FASO
Ouagadougou
Wadi Halfa
Port Sudan
Atbara
El Khartum
Wad Medani
El Obeid
Bahr el Arab
SUDAN
Wau
ERITREA
Asmera
San'a
REP. OF YEMEN
Gulf of Aden
DJIBOUTI
Djibouti
Adis Abeba
ETHIOPIA

Bissau
GUINEA
Conakry
Kankan
SIERRA LEONE
Freetown
Monrovia
LIBERIA
Yamoussoukro
CÔTE D'IVOIRE
GHANA
BENIN
Abidjan
Accra
Lomé
TOGO
Porto Novo
Ibadan
Lagos
Ogbomosho
NIGERIA
Abuja
Enugu
CENTRAL AFRICAN REPUBLIC
Bangui
Bangassou
CAMEROON
Douala
Yaoundé
Ngaoundéré
Zaïre
Wau
Jûbâ
Turkana
UGANDA
Kampala
L. Victoria
Kisangani
Nairobi
KENYA
Kismaayo
SOMALIA
Muqdisho

Equator
Gulf of Guinea
Malabo
Bata
EQUAT. GUINEA
SÃO TOMÉ & PRÍNCIPE
São Tomé
Annobon
Libreville
GABON
CONGO
Congo
Mbandaka
DEMOCRATIC REPUBLIC OF CONGO
Kananga
Kindu
RWANDA
Kigali
BURUNDI
Bujumbura
Kigoma
Mwanza
L. Tanganyika
Arusha
Dodoma
Mombasa
Zanzibar
Dar es Salaam
TANZANIA

Ascension Island (U.K.)
Pointe Noire
Brazzaville
Kinshasa
CABINDA (Angola)
Luanda
Malanje
Kasai
Kalemie
Kamina
Likasi
Lubumbashi
Ndola
Mbeya
L. Malawi
MALAWI
COMOROS
Pemba
Antsiranana

ATLANTIC OCEAN
St. Helena (U.K.)
Lobito
Huambo
Lubango
Namibe
ANGOLA
ZAMBIA
Lusaka
Zambezi
Lilongwe
Lichinga
Blantyre
MOZAMBIQUE
Nampula
Moçambique
Mozambique Channel
MADAGASCAR
Antananarivo

Tsumeb
Livingstone
ZIMBABWE
Harare
Bulawayo
Limpopo
Beira
Inhambane
Toliara

Walvis Bay
Windhoek
NAMIBIA
Keetmanshoop
BOTSWANA
Gaborone
Pretoria
Johannesburg
Maputo
Mbabane
SWAZILAND

of Capricorn
Orange
Bloemfontein
Maseru
LESOTHO
Durban
East London
SOUTH AFRICA
Cape Town
Port Elizabeth
INDIAN OCEAN

Tristan da Cunha (U.K.)
West of Greenwich 0° East of Greenwich 10° 20° 30° 40° 50°

Scale 1:48 000 000

| 0 | 400 | 800 | 1200 | 1600 km |

| 0 | 250 | 500 | 750 | 1000 miles |

42

Scale 1:23 500 000

```
0     200    400    600    800 km
```

```
0    100   200   300   400   500 miles
```

© Geddes & Grosset

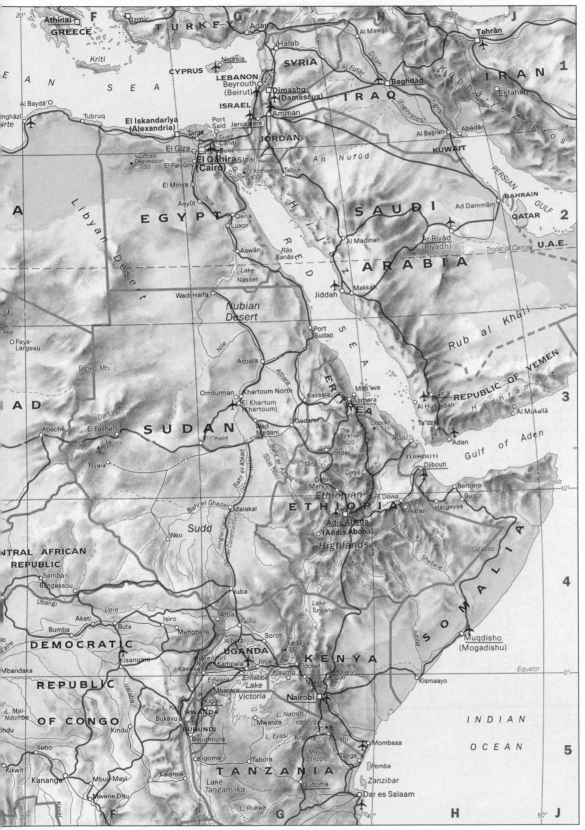

43

44

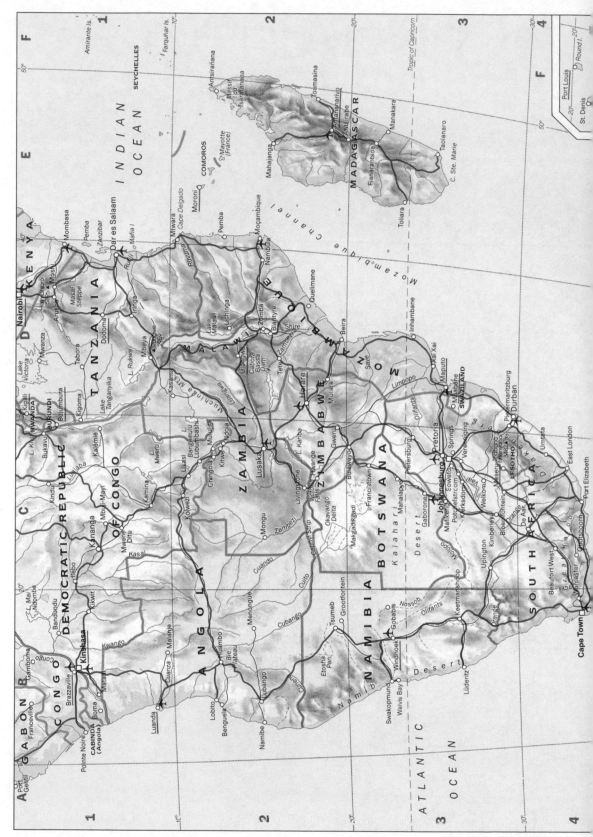

Scale 1:23 500 000

```
0     200    400    600    800 km
```

```
0    100   200   300   400   500 miles
```

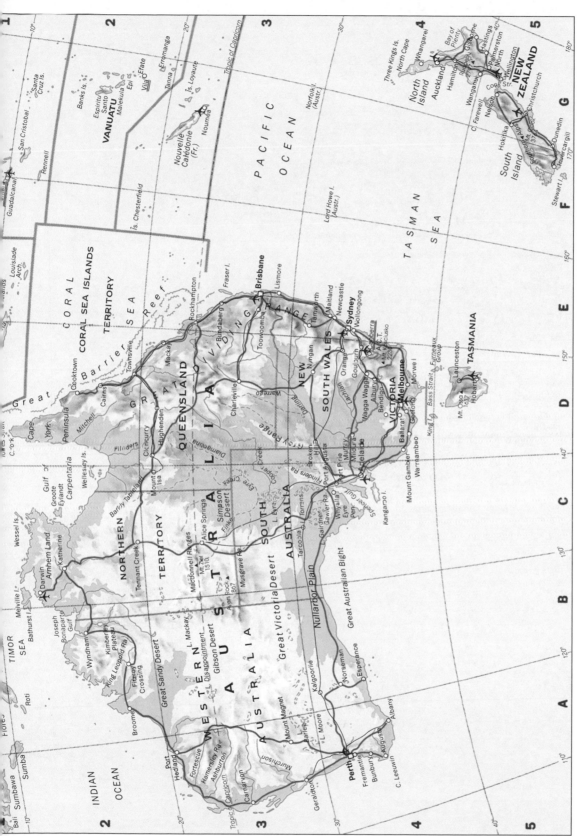

45

Scale 1:29 000 000

0   200   400   600   800   1000 km

0   200   400   600 miles

46

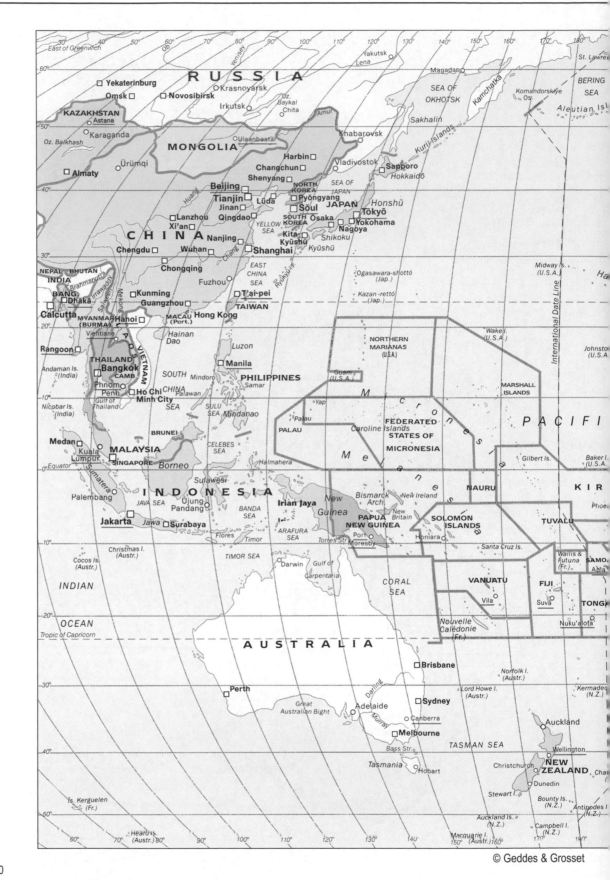

Scale 1:72 000 000

| 0 | 1000 | 2000 | 3000 km |

| 0 | 500 | 1000 | 1500 | 2000 miles |

© Geddes & Grosset

47

A
Anchorage
Gulf of Alaska
Kodiak I.
Alexander Arch.
Queen Charlotte Is.
Vancouver I.
Great Bear Lake
Mackenzie
Great Slave Lake
L. Athabasca
Edmonton
Calgary
Regina
L. Winnipeg
Winnipeg
CANADA
Hudson Bay
Davis Str.
GREENLAND (Den.)
ICELAND
Reykjavik
West of Greenwich
LABRADOR SEA
Newfoundland

Vancouver
Seattle
Portland
Missouri
Snake
L. Superior
Minneapolis
L. Michigan
L. Huron
Chicago
Detroit
Pittsburgh
Denver
Cincinnati
St. Louis
Ohio
Washington
UNITED STATES
L. Ontario
L. Erie
Montréal
Ottawa
Toronto
Boston
New York
Philadelphia
Baltimore
St. Lawrence
ATLANTIC

San Francisco
Los Angeles
San Diego
Colorado
OF AMERICA
Dallas
Rio Grande
Rio Bravo del Norte
Mississippi
Atlanta
New Orleans
Houston
Bermuda (U.K.)
OCEAN

Guadalupe (Mex.)
Monterrey
GULF OF MEXICO
Miami
THE BAHAMAS
Tropic of Cancer
MEXICO
La Habana
CUBA
DOMINICAN REPUBLIC

Honolulu
Hawaii
Revillagigedo (Mex.)
Guadalajara
México
BELIZE
GUATEMALA
Guatemala
San Salvador
EL SALVADOR
Tegucigalpa
HONDURAS
NICARAGUA
Managua
JAMAICA
Greater Antilles
HAITI
Puerto Rico (U.S.A.)
CARIBBEAN SEA
Lesser Antilles

OCEAN
Tabuaeran
Kiritimati
myra (S.A.)
arvis I. (U.S.A.)
Malden I.
Starbuck I.
Caroline I.
Flint I.
Clipperton I. (Fr.)
COSTA RICA
San José
PANAMA
Panamá
de Coco (C.R.)
Caracas
VENEZUELA
Medellín
Bogotá
COLOMBIA

Îs. Marquises (Fr.)
Îs. de la Société (Fr.)
Tahiti
Îs. Tuamotu (Fr.)
FRENCH POLYNESIA
Islas Galápagos (Ecuador)
Equator
Quito
Guayaquil
ECUADOR
Amazonas
Trujillo
BRAZIL
PERU
Callao
Lima

Îs. Tubuai (Fr.)
Îs. Gambier
Pitcairn I. (U.K.)
Ducie I.
Sala-y-Gomez (Ch.)
I. de Pascua (Ch.)
Arequipa
L. Titicaca
La Paz
BOLIVIA
Sucre
Tropic of Capricorn
Antofagasta
PAR.
Asunción

Is. Juan Fernández (Ch.)
Santiago
CHILE
Concepción
ARGENTINA
Córdoba
Rosario
Buenos Aires
URUGUAY
Montevideo
Bahía Blanca
Puerto Montt
Patagonia
Punta Arenas
Tierra del Fuego
Falkland Is. (Islas Malvinas) (U.K.)
South Georgia (U.K.)

150° 140° 130° 120° 110° 100° 90° 80° 70° 60° 50° 40° 30° 20° 10° 0° 10°
60° 50° 40° 30° 20° 10° 0°

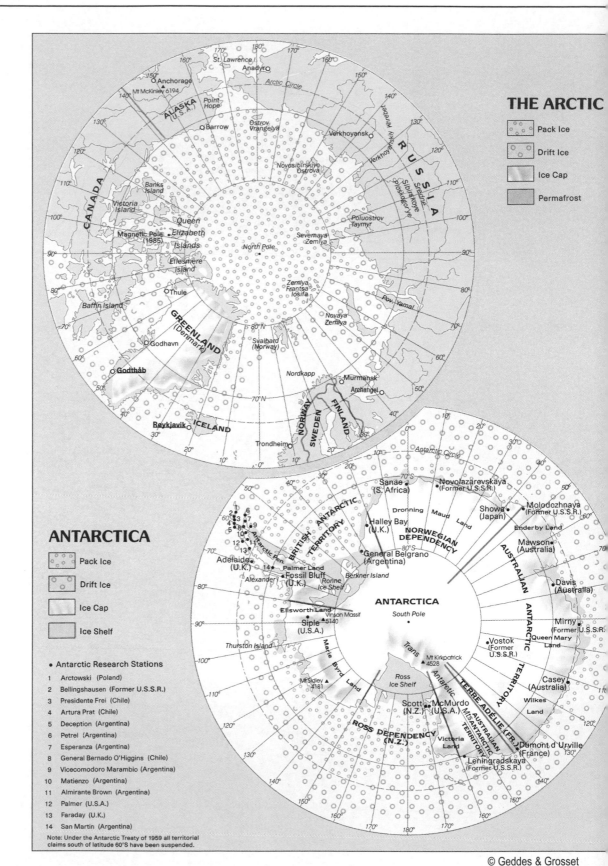

THE ARCTIC

- Pack Ice
- Drift Ice
- Ice Cap
- Permafrost

ANTARCTICA

- Pack Ice
- Drift Ice
- Ice Cap
- Ice Shelf

• Antarctic Research Stations

1 Arctowski (Poland)
2 Bellingshausen (Former U.S.S.R.)
3 Presidente Frei (Chile)
4 Artura Prat (Chile)
5 Deception (Argentina)
6 Petrel (Argentina)
7 Esperanza (Argentina)
8 General Bernado O'Higgins (Chile)
9 Vicecomodoro Marambio (Argentina)
10 Matienzo (Argentina)
11 Almirante Brown (Argentina)
12 Palmer (U.S.A.)
13 Faraday (U.K.)
14 San Martin (Argentina)

Note: Under the Antarctic Treaty of 1959 all territorial claims south of latitude 60°S have been suspended.

© Geddes & Grosset

Scale 1:60 000 000

0 400 800 1200 1600 km

0 200 400 600 800 1000 miles

Index

Berbera *Somalia* 43H3
Bergarno *Italy* 26B1
Bergen *Norway* 30B3
Berkner I. *Antarctica* 48
Berlin *Germany* 28C2
Bermuda I. *Atlantic Ocean* 7G2
Bern *Switzerland* 24D2
Berry *Province France* 24C2
Berwick-upon-Tweed *England* 20E2
Besançon *France* 24D2
Betanzos *Spain* 25A1
Beverley *England* 20G4
Beyla *Guinea* 42C4
Beyrouth (Beirut) *Lebanon* 38B2
Béziers *France* 24C3
Bhagalpur *India* 39G3
Bhamo *Myanmar* 36B1
Bhopal *India* 39F3
Bhutan 39G/H3
Biak I. *Indonesia* 37F4
Bialystok *Poland* 29E2
Bideford *England* 21C6
Biel *Switzerland* 24D2
Bikaner *India* 39F3
Bilaspur *India* 39G3
Bilbao *Spain* 25B1
Billings *USA* 6C1
Bioko I. *Atlantic Ocean* 42D4
Birkenhead *England* 20D4
Bîrlad *Romania* 29F3
Birmingham *England* 21F5
Birmingham *USA* 7E2
Bir Moghrein *Mauritania* 42B2
Birobidzhan *Russia* 33P5
Birr *Ireland* 23D3
Bishkek *Kyrgyzstan* 32J5
Bishop Auckland *England* 20F3
Biskra *Algeria* 42D1
Bismarck Arch. *Pacific Ocean* 37H4
Bismarck *USA* 6C1
Bissau *Guinea-Bissau* 42B3
Bitola *Macedonia* 27E2
Bizerte *Tunisia* 42D1
Blace *Croatia* 27D2
Blackburn *England* 20E4
Blackpool *England* 20D4
Blagoveshchensk *Russia* 33O4
Blagoevgrad *Bulgaria* 27E2
Blair Atholl *Scotland* 22E4
Blantyre *Malawi* 44D2
Blida *Algeria* 42D1
Bloemfontein *South Africa* 44C3
Blönduós *Iceland* 30A1
Bluefields *Nicaragua* 14C4
Blyth *England* 20F2
Bo *Sierra Leone* 42B4
Boa Vista *Brazil* 16C2
Bobo Dioulasso *Burkina Faso* 42C3
Bocas del Toro *Panama* 14C5
Boden *Sweden* 30E2
Bodmin *England* 21C7
Bodö *Norway* 30C2
Bodrum *Turkey* 27F3
Bognor Regis *England* 21G7
Bogor *Indonesia* 36C4
Bogotá *Colombia* 16B2
Bohol *Philippines* 37E3
Boise *USA* 6B1
Boké *Guinea* 42B3
Bolivia 16C4
Bollnäs *Sweden* 30D3
Bologna *Italy* 26C2
Bolton *England* 20E4
Boma *Dem. Rep. of Congo* 42E5
Bombay *India* 39F4
Bonaire *Caribbean Sea* 14F4
Bonn *Germany* 28B2
Boothia Peninsula *Canada* 5J2
Borås *Sweden* 30C4
Bordeaux *France* 24B3
Borneo *Indonesia/Malaysia* 36D3
Bornholm I. *Denmark* 30C4
Borzya *Russia* 33N4
Bosanski Brod *Croatia* 27D1
Bosnia Herzegovina 27D2
Boston *England* 20G5
Boston *USA* 7F1
Botswana 44C3
Bouaké *Côte d'Ivoire* 42C4
Bouar *Central African Republic* 42E4
Bouârfa *Morocco* 42C1
Boulogne *France* 24C1
Bounty Is. *New Zealand* 46
Bourg-en-Bresse *France* 24D2
Bourges *France* 24C2
Bourgogne (Burgundy) *Province France* 24C2
Bournemouth *England* 21F7
Boyle *Ireland* 23C3
Brac I. *Croatia* 26D2
Bräcke *Sweden* 30D3
Bradford *England* 20F4
Braga *Portugal* 25A1
Braila *Romania* 39F3
Brasília *Brazil* 16E4
Brasov *Romania* 29F3
Bratislava *Slovakia* 28D3
Bratsk *Russia* 33M4
Braunschweig *Germany* 28C2
Bray *Ireland* 23E3
Brazil 16B/F4
Brazzaville *Congo* 42E5
Breda *Netherlands* 28A2
Bremen *Germany* 28B2
Bremerhaven *Germany* 28B2
Brescia *Italy* 26C1
Bressay *Scotland* 22J7
Bressuire *France* 24B2
Brest *France* 24B2
Brest *Belarus* 29E2
Bretagne (Brittany) *Province France* 24B2
Briançon *France* 24D3
Briare *France* 24C2
Bridgetown *Barbados* 14H4
Bridgwater *England* 21D6
Bridlington *England* 20G3
Brighton *England* 21G7
Brindisi *Italy* 27D2
Brisbane *Australia* 45E3
Bristol *England* 21E6
British Columbia *Province Canada* 5F4
Brittany *see* Bretagne 24B2
Brive-la-Gaillarde *France* 24C2
Brno *Czech Republic* 28D3
Broken Hill *Australia* 45D/E4
Broome *Australia* 45B2
Brora *Scotland* 22E2
Brownsville *USA* 6D3
Bruck an der Mur *Austria* 28D3
Brunei, Sultanate *SE Asia* 36D3
Brussels *see* Bruxelles 24C1
Bruxelles (Brussels) *Belgium* 24C1
Bryansk *Russia* 32E4
Bucaramanga *Colombia* 16B2
Buchanan *Liberia* 42B4
Bucharest *see* Bucuresti 27F2
Buckie *Scotland* 22F3
Buckingham *England* 21F6
Bucuresti (Bucharest) *Romania* 27F2
Budapest *Hungary* 29D3
Bude *England* 21C7
Buenaventura *Colombia* 16B2
Buenos Aires *Argentina* 17C/D6
Buenos Aires *State Argentina* 17C6
Buffalo *New York State, USA* 7F1
Buffalo *Wyoming, USA* 6C1
Builth Wells *Wales* 21D5
Bujumbura *Burundi* 43F5
Bukavu *Dem. Rep. of Congo* 43F5
Bukhara *Uzbekistan* 32H6
Bukittinggi *Indonesia* 36C4
Bulawayo *Zimbabwe* 44C3
Bulgaria 27E2
Bumba *Dem. Rep. of Congo* 43F4
Bunbury *Australia* 45A4
Bundaberg *Australia* 45E3
Bundoran *Ireland* 23C2
Buraydah *Saudi Arabia* 38C3
Burco *Somalia* 43H4
Burgas *Bulgaria* 27F2
Burgos *Spain* 25B1
Burgundy *see* Bourgogne 24C2
Burkina Faso 42C/D3
Burley *USA* 6B1
Burma *see* Myanmar 36B/C1
Bursa *Turkey* 38A1
Buru I. *Indonesia* 37E4
Burundi 43F/G5
Bury St Edmunds *England* 21H5
Buta *Dem. Rep. of Congo* 43F4
Bute *Scotland* 22C5
Butte *USA* 6B1
Butuan *Philippines* 37E3
Butung I. *Indonesia* 37E4
Buzau *Romania* 29F3
Byala *Bulgaria* 27F2
Bydgoszcz *Poland* 29D2
Bylot I. *Canada* 5K/L2
Bytom *Poland* 29D2

C

Cabanatuan *Philippines* 37E2
Cabimas *Venezuela* 16B1
Cabinda *Angola* 42E5
Cacak *Yugoslavia* 27E2
Cáceres *Spain* 25A2
Cádiz *Spain* 25A2
Caen *France* 24B2
Caernarfon *Wales* 20C4
Cagayan de Oro *Philippines* 37E3
Cagliari *Italy* 26B3
Caher *Ireland* 23D4
Cahors *France* 24C3
Caicos Is. *Caribbean Sea* 14E2
Cairns *Australia* 45D2
Cairo *see* El Qâhira 43G1
Calahorra *Spain* 25B1
Calais *France* 24C1
Calama *Chile* 17B5
Calamian Group *Philippines* 36D2
Calatayud *Spain* 25B1
Calcutta *India* 39G3
Calgary *Canada* 5G4
Cali *Colombia* 16B2
California *State USA* 6A/B2
Callao *Peru* 16B4
Calvi *France* 26B2
Camagüey *Cuba* 14D2
Cambodia 36C2
Cambridge *England* 21H5
Camden *USA* 7F2
Cameroon 42E4
Campbell I. *New Zealand* 46
Campbeltown *Scotland* 22C5
Campinas *Brazil* 16E5
Campo Grande *Brazil* 16D5
Campos *Brazil* 17E5
Canada 5
Canary Is. *see* Islas Canarias 42B2
Canberra *Australia* 45D4
Cangzjou *China* 35F3
Cannes *France* 24D3
Canterbury *England* 21J6
Can Tho *Vietnam* 36C3
Cape Breton I. *Canada* 5M5
Cape Town *South Africa* 44B4
Cape Verde Is. 2
Cap-Haïtien *Haiti* 14E3
Capri I. *Italy* 26C2
Caracal *Romania* 27E2
Caracaraí *Brazil* 16C2
Caracas *Venezuela* 16C1
Caransebes *Romania* 29E3
Carbonia *Italy* 26B3
Carcassonne *France* 24C3
Cardiff *Wales* 21D6
Cardigan *Wales* 21C5
Carlisle *England* 20E3
Carlow *Ireland* 23E4
Carmarthen *Wales* 21C6
Carnarvon *Australia* 45A3
Carolina *Brazil* 16E3
Caroline I. *Kiribati* 46
Caroline Is. *Pacific Ocean* 37G3
Carrick-on-Shannon *Ireland* 23C3
Carrickmacross *Ireland* 23E3
Carson City *USA* 6B2
Cartagena *Colombia* 16B1
Cartagena *Spain* 25B2
Cartago *Costa Rica* 14C5
Caserta *Italy* 26C2
Cashel *Ireland* 23D4
Casper *USA* 6C1
Cassino *Italy* 26C2
Castellón de la Plana *Spain* 25B2
Castilla La Mancha *Region Spain* 25B2
Castilla y León *Region Spain* 25A/B1
Castlebar *Ireland* 23B3
Castleford *England* 20F4
Castries *St Lucia* 14G4
Castrovillari *Italy* 26D3
Cataluña *Region Spain* 25C1
Catamarca *State Argentina* 16C5
Catania *Italy* 26D3
Catanzaro *Italy* 26D3
Cateraggio *France* 26B2
Cat I. *The Bahamas* 14D2
Cavan *Ireland* 23D2/3
Cayenne *French Guiana* 16D2
Cayman Is. *Caribbean Sea* 14C3
Ceará *State Brazil* 16F3
Cebu I. *Philippines* 37E2
Cebu *Philippines* 37E2
Cecina *Italy* 26C2
Cefalû *Italy* 26C3
Central African Republic 43E/F4
Cerignola *Italy* 26D2
Ceské Budejovice *Czech Republic* 28C3
Ceuta *Spain* 25A2
Ch'ongjin *North Korea* 35G2
Chaco *State Argentina* 16C/D5
Chad 43E/F3
Chalon-sur-Saône *France* 24D2
Châlons-sur-Marne *France* 24C2
Chambéry *France* 24D2
Champagne *Province France* 24C2
Chañaral *Chile* 17B5
Chandigarh *India* 39F2
Chang-hua *Taiwan* 37E1
Changchun *China* 35G2
Changde *China* 35F4
Changsha *China* 35F4
Changzhi *China* 35F3
Channel Is. *UK* 21E8
Channel Port-aux-Basques *Canada* 5N5
Chardzhou *Turkmenistan* 32H6
Charleroi *Belgium* 24C1
Charleston *USA* 7F2
Charleville *Australia* 45D3
Charlotte *USA* 7E2
Charlottetown *Canada* 5M5
Chartres *France* 24C2
Châteauroux *France* 24C2
Chatham Is. *New Zealand* 46
Chattanooga *USA* 7E2
Chaumont *France* 24D2
Chaves *Port.* 25A1
Cheboksary *Russia* 32F4
Cheju do I. *South Korea* 35G3
Chelmsford *England* 21H6
Cheltenham *England* 21E6
Chelyabinsk *Russia* 32H4
Chemnitz *Germany* 28C2
Chen Xian *China* 35F4
Chengdu *China* 34E3
Cherbourg *France* 24B2
Cheremkhovo *Russia* 33M4
Cherepovets *Russia* 32E4
Chernigov *Ukraine* 32F4
Chernovtsy *Ukraine* 32D5
Chesham *England* 21G6
Chester *England* 20E4
Chesterfield Inlet *Canada* 5J3
Chetumal *Mexico* 14B3
Cheyenne *USA* 6C1
Chiang Mai *Thailand* 36B2
Chiba *Japan* 35P9
Chicago *USA* 7E1
Chichester *England* 21G7
Chiclayo *Peru* 16B3
Chifeng *China* 35F2
Chihuahua *Mexico* 6C3
Chile 17B5/6
Chi-lung *Taiwan* 37E1
Chimbote *Peru* 16B3
Chimkent *Kazakhstan* 32H5
China 34/35
Chingola *Zambia* 44C2
Chippenham *England* 21E6
Chita *Russia* 33N4
Chittagong *Bangladesh* 39H3
Chojnice *Poland* 28D2
Chongqing *China* 34E4
Chorley *England* 20E4
Choybalsan *Mongolia* 35F2
Christchurch *New Zealand* 45G5
Christmas I. *Indian Ocean* 36C5
Chubut *State Argentina* 17C7
Chumphon *Thailand* 36B2
Church Stretton *England* 21E5
Churchill *Canada* 5J4
Cienfuegos *Cuba* 14C2
Cieza *Spain* 25B2
Cîmpina *Romania* 29F3
Cincinnati *USA* 7E2
Cirebon *Indonesia* 36C4
Citta di Castello *Italy* 26C2
Ciudad Bolivar *Venezuela* 16C2
Ciudad Guayana *Venezuela* 16C2
Ciudad Juárez *Mexico* 6C2
Ciudad Real *Spain* 25B2
Ciudad Rodrigo *Spain* 25A1
Civitanova Marche *Italy* 26C2
Civitavecchia *Italy* 26C2
Clacton-on-Sea *England* 21J6
Clare I. *Ireland* 23A3
Claremorris *Ireland* 23B3
Clermont Ferrand *France* 24C2
Cleveland *USA* 7E1
Clifden *Ireland* 23A3
Cloghan *Ireland* 23D3
Cloncurry *Australia* 45D2
Clonmel *Ireland* 23D4
Cluj-Napoca *Romania* 29E3
Coatbridge *Scotland* 22D5
Cobán *Guatemala* 14A3
Cobh *Ireland* 23C5
Cochabamba *Bolivia* 16C4
Cochin *India* 39F5
Cocos I. *Indian Ocean* 36B5
Codó *Brazil* 16E3
Coimbatore *India* 39F4
Coimbra *Portugal* 25A1
Colchester *England* 21H6
Coleraine *Northern Ireland* 23E1
Coll I. *Scotland* 22B4
Collooney *Ireland* 23C2
Colmar *France* 24D2
Cologne *see* Köln 28B2
Colombia 16B2
Colombo *Sri Lanka* 39F5
Colombus *USA* 7E2
Colón *Panama* 14D5
Colonsay I. *Scotland* 22B4
Colorado *State USA* 6C2
Colorada Springs *USA* 6C2
Columbia *USA* 7E2
Columbus *USA* 7E2
Como *Italy* 26B1
Comodoro Rivadavia *Argentina* 17C7
Comoros Is. *Indian Ocean* 44E2
Compiègne *France* 24C2
Conakry *Guinea* 42B4
Concepción *Chile* 17B6
Concepción *Paraguay* 17D5
Concord *USA* 7F1
Concordia *Argentina* 17D6
Congo, Republic of the 42E5
Connecticut *State USA* 7F1
Consett *England* 20F3
Constanta *Romania* 27F2
Constantine *Algeria* 42D1
Contonou *Benin* 42D4
Cook Is. *Pacific Ocean* 47
Cooktown *Australia* 45D2
Copenhagen *see* København 30C4
Corby *England* 21G5
Corcubíon *Spain* 25A1
Córdoba *Argentina* 17C6
Córdoba *Spain* 25B2
Cordoba *State Argentina* 17C6
Corfu I. *Greece* 27D3
Corigliano *Italy* 26D3
Corinth *see* Kórinthos 27E3
Corinto *Nicaragua* 14B4
Cork *Ireland* 23C5
Coro *Venezuela* 16C1
Corpus Christi *USA* 6D3
Corrientes *Argentina* 17D5
Corrientes *State Argentina* 17D5
Corse I. (Corsica) *France* 26B2
Corumbá *Brazil* 16D4
Cosenza *Italy* 26D3
Costa Rica 14C5
Cotabato *Philippines* 37E3
Cottbus *Germany* 28C2
Coventry *England* 21F5
Cowes *Isle of Wight* 21F7
Craiova *Romania* 27E2
Crawley *England* 21G6
Cres I. *Croatia* 26C2
Crete I. *Greece* 27E3
Crewe *England* 20E4
Crianlarich *Scotland* 22D4
Crieff *Scotland* 22E4
Cromer *England* 21J5
Crotone *Italy* 26D3
Cruzeiro do Sul *Brazil* 16B3
Cuba 14C/D2
Cucuí *Brazil* 16C2
Cúcuta *Colombia* 16B2
Cuddalore *India* 39F4
Cuenca *Ecuador* 16B3
Cuenca *Spain* 25B1
Cuiabá *Brazil* 16D4
Culiacán *Mexico* 6C3
Cumbernauld *Scotland* 22D5
Cumnock *Scotland* 22D5
Cuneo *Italy* 26B2
Cupar *Scotland* 22E4
Curaçao *Caribbean Sea* 14F4
Curitiba *Brazil* 16E5
Cuttack *India* 39G3
Cuxhaven *Germany* 28B2
Cuzco *Peru* 16B4
Cwmbran *Wales* 21D6
Cyprus 40B1
Czech Republic 28D3
Czestochowa *Poland* 29C3/D2

D

Dacca *see* Dhaka 39H3
Dagupan *Philippines* 37E2
Dakar *Senegal* 42B3
Da Lat *Vietnam* 36C2
Dali *China* 34E4
Dallas *USA* 6D2
Dalmally *Scotland* 22D4
Daloa *Côte d'Ivoire* 42C4
Damascus *see* Dimashq 38B2
Da Nang *Vietnam* 36C2
Dandong *China* 35G2
Dar'a *Syria* 38B2
Dar el Beida *Morocco* 42C1
Dar es Salaam *Tanzania* 43G5
Darlington *England* 20F3
Darmstadt *Germany* 28B3
Daroca *Spain* 25B1
Daru *Papua New Guinea* 37G4
Darwin *Australia* 45C2
Datong *China* 35F2
Daugavpils *Latvia* 32D4
Dauphine *Province France* 24D3
Davao *Philippines* 37E3
David *Panama* 14C5
Dawson Creek *Canada* 5F4
Dax *France* 24B3
Dayton *USA* 7E2
Daytona Beach *USA* 7E3
De Aar *South Africa* 44C4
Debre Mark'os *Ethiopia* 43G3

Debrecen *Hungary* 29E3
Dehra Dun *India* 39F2
Delaware *State USA* 7F2
Delhi *India* 39F3
Democratic Republic of Congo 43F5
Denbigh *Wales* 20D4
Den Helder *Netherlands* 28A2
Denizli *Turkey* 38A2
Denmark 30C4
D'Entrecasteaux I. *Papua New Guinea* 37H4
Denver *USA* 6C2
Derby *England* 21F5
Dese *Ethiopia* 43G3
Des Moines *USA* 7D1
Dessau *Germany* 28C2
Detroit *USA* 7E1
Deva *Romania* 29E3
Devon I. *Canada* 5K2
Dezful *Iran* 38C2
Dezhou *China* 35F3
Dhaka (Dacca) *Bangladesh* 39H3
Dibrugarh *India* 39H3
Didcot *England* 21F6
Dieppe *France* 24C2
Dijon *France* 24D2
Dili *Indonesia* 37E4
Dimashq (Damascus) *Syria* 38C2
Dimitrovgrad *Bulgaria* 27F2
Dingle *Ireland* 23A4
Dingwall *Scotland* 22D3
Dire Dawa *Ethiopia* 43H4
Disko I. *Greenland* 5N3
Dist. Fed. *State Brazil* 16E4
Diyarbakir *Turkey* 38B2
Djelfa *Algeria* 42D1
Djibouti *Djibouti* 43H3
Dnepropetrovsk *Ukraine* 32E5
Dobreta-Turnu-Severin *Romania* 27E2
Dodoma *Tanzania* 43G5
Dôle *France* 24D2
Dolgellau *Wales* 21D5
Dombås *Norway* 30B3
Dominica I. *Caribbean* 14G3
Dominican Republic 14F3
Domodossola *Italy* 26B1
Doncaster *England* 20F4
Donegal *Ireland* 23C/D2
Donetsk *Ukraine* 32E5
Dorchester *England* 21E7
Dornie *Scotland* 22C3
Dortmund *Germany* 28B2
Douala *Cameroon* 42D4
Douglas *Isle of Man* 20C3
Dourados *Brazil* 17D5
Dover *England* 21J6
Dover *USA* 7F2
Dráma *Greece* 27E2
Drammen *Norway* 30C4
Dresden *Germany* 28C2
Drogheda *Ireland* 23E3
Dubayy *United Arab Emirates* 38D3
Dublin *Ireland* 23E3
Dubrovnik *Croatia* 27D2
Ducie I. *Pacific Ocean* 47
Dudley *England* 21E5
Dugi I. *Croatia* 26C/D2
Duisburg *Germany* 28B2
Dukou *China* 34D4
Duluth *USA* 7D1
Dumbarton *Scotland* 22D5
Dumfries *Scotland* 22E5
Dunbar *Scotland* 22F5
Dundalk *Ireland* 23E2
Dundee *Scotland* 22F4
Dundrum *Northern Ireland* 23F2
Dunedin *New Zealand* 45G5
Dunfermline *Scotland* 22E4
Dungarvan *Ireland* 23D4
Dungiven *Northern Ireland* 23E2
Dunkeld *Scotland* 22E4
Dunkerque *France* 24C1
Dun Laoghaire *Ireland* 23E3
Dunleer *Ireland* 23E3
Durban *South Africa* 44D3
Durham *England* 20F3
Durham *USA* 7F2
Durness *Scotland* 22D2
Durrës *Albania* 27D2
Durrow *Ireland* 23D4
Dushanbe *Tajikistan* 32H6
Dusseldorf *Germany* 28B2
Duyun *China* 34E4

E

Eastbourne *England* 21H7
East Falkland I. *South Atlantic Ocean* 17D8
East Kilbride *Scotland* 22D5
East London *South Africa* 44C4
Eboli *Italy* 26D2
Ecija *Spain* 25A2
Ecuador 16B3
Eday I. *Scotland* 22F1
Edgeworthstown *Ireland* 23D3
Edinburgh *Scotland* 22E5
Edmonton *Canada* 5G4
Efate I. *Vanuatu* 45F2
Egadi I. *Italy* 26C3
Egersund *Norway* 30B4
Egypt 43F/G2
Eigg I. *Scotland* 22B4
Eindhoven *Netherlands* 28B2
Eisenach *Germany* 28C2
Elba I. *Italy* 26C2
Elblag *Poland* 29D2
Elche *Spain* 25B2
El Dorado *Venezuela* 16C2
Eldoret *Kenya* 43G4
Eleuthera I. *The Bahamas* 14D1
El Faiyûm *Egypt* 43G2
El Fasher *Sudan* 43F3
El Ferrol *Spain* 25A1
Elgin *Scotland* 22E3
El Gîza *Egypt* 43G1
El Golea *Algeria* 42D1
El Iskandarîya (Alexandria) *Egypt* 43F1
El Khartum (Khartoum) *Sudan* 43G3
Ellesmere I. *Canada* 5K2
Ellesmere Port *England* 20E4
Ellon *Scotland* 22F3
El Minya *Egypt* 43G2
El Obeid *Sudan* 43G3
El Paso *USA* 6C2
El Qâhira (Cairo) *Egypt* 43G1
El Salvador 14B4
Elvas *Portugal* 25A2
Ely *England* 21H5
Enarración *Paraguay* 17D5
Ende *Indonesia* 37E4
Enggano I. *Indonesia* 36C4
Enna *Italy* 26C3
Ennis *Ireland* 23B4
Enniscorthy *Ireland* 23E4
Enniskillen *Northern Ireland* 23D2
Ennistymon *Ireland* 23B4
Enschede *Netherlands* 28B2
Entebbe *Uganda* 43G4
Enugu *Nigeria* 42D4
Epi I. *Vanuatu* 45F2
Equatorial Guinea 42F4
Erenhot *China* 35F2
Erfurt *Germany* 28C2
Eriskay I. *Scotland* 22A3
Erlangen *Germany* 28C3
Erromanga I. *Vanuatu* 45F2
Erzurum *Turkey* 38C2
Esbjerg *Denmark* 30B4
Esfahan *Iran* 38D2
Eskisehir *Turkey* 38B2
Esperance *Australia* 45B4
Espírito Santo *Brazil* 16E4
Espiritu Santo I. *Vanuatu* 45F2
Espoo *Finland* 30E3
Essaouira *Morocco* 42C1
Essen *Germany* 28B2
Estonia 30F4
Estremoz *Portugal* 25A2
Ethiopia 43G/H4
Evansville *USA* 7E2
Evvoia I. *Greece* 27E3
Exeter *England* 21D7
Extremadura *Region Spain* 25A2

F

Faeroes Is. (Føroyar Is.) *Denmark* 30A2
Fair I. *Scotland* 22J8
Fairbanks *USA* 6J
Faisalabad *Pakistan* 39F2
Fakfak *Indonesia* 37F4
Falcarragh *Ireland* 23C1
Falkirk *Scotland* 22E4
Falkland Islands *South Atlantic Ocean* 17C/D8
Falmouth *England* 21B7
Falster I. *Denmark* 30C5
Falun *Sweden* 30D3
Fano *Italy* 26C2
Farah *Afghanistan* 38E2
Fareham *England* 21F7
Fargo *USA* 6D1
Faro *Portugal* 25A2
Farquhar Is. *Indian Ocean* 44F1
Fauske *Norway* 30D2
Faya-Largeau *Chad* 43E3
Fdérik *Mauritania* 42B2
Felixstowe *England* 21J6
Fergana *Uzbekistan* 32J5
Ferkessédougou *Côte d'Ivoire* 42C4
Fermoy *Ireland* 23C4
Ferrara *Italy* 26C2
Fès *Morocco* 42C1
Fetlar I. *Scotland* 22K7
Feyzabad *Afghanistan* 39F2
Fianarantsoa *Madagascar* 44E3
Figueras *Spain* 25C1
Fiji Is. *Pacific Ocean* 46
Filiasi *Romania* 27E2
Finland 30E3/F3
Firenze (Florence) *Italy* 26C2
Fishguard *Wales* 21C6
Fitzroy Crossing *Australia* 45B2
Fleetwood *England* 20D4
Flensburg *Germany* 28B2
Flint I. *Kiribati* 477
Florence *see* Firenze 26C2
Flores *Guatemala* 14B3
Flores I. *Indonesia* 37E4
Florianópolis *Brazil* 16E5
Florida *State USA* 7E3
Focsani *Romania* 29F3
Foggia *Italy* 26D2
Foligno *Italy* 26C2
Follonica *Italy* 26C2
Forfar *Scotland* 22F4
Forli *Italy* 26C2
Formentera I. *Spain* 25C2
Formia *Italy* 26C2
Formosa *State Argentina* 16C/D5
Føroyar Is. *see* Faeroes Is. 30A2
Fortaleza *Brazil* 16F3
Fort Augustus *Scotland* 22D3
Fort-de-France *Martinique* 14G4
Fort Lauderdale *USA* 7E3
Fort Simpson *Canada* 5F3
Fort William *Scotland* 22C4
Fort Worth *USA* 6D2
Fort Yukon *USA* 5D3
Foshan *China* 35F4
Fougères *France* 24B2
Foula I. *Scotland* 22H7
Foz do Iguaçu *Brazil* 17D5
Fraga *Spain* 25C1
Franca *Brazil* 16E5
France 24
Franceville *Gabon* 42E5
Franche-Comte *Province France* 24D2
Francistown *Botswana* 44C3
Frankfort *USA* 7E2
Frankfurt *Germany* 28B2
Fraser I. *Australia* 45E3
Fraserburgh *Scotland* 22F3
Frederikshåb *Greenland* 5O3
Frederikshavn *Denmark* 30C4
Frederikstad *Norway* 30C4
Freetown *Sierra Leone* 42B4
Freiburg *Germany* 28B3
Fremantle *Australia* 45A4
Fresno *USA* 6B2
Frosinone *Italy* 26C2
Ft. Wayne *USA* 7E1
Fuerteventura I. *Canary Islands* 42B2
Fujian *Province China* 35F4
Fukui *Japan* 35M8
Fukuoka *Japan* 35H3
Fukushima *Japan* 35P8
Funchal *Madeira* 42B1
Furneaux Group I. *Australia* 45D5
Fürth *Germany* 28C3
Furukawa *Japan* 35P7
Fushun *China* 35G2
Fuxin *China* 35G2
Fuzhou *China* 35F4
Fyn I. *Denmark* 30C4

G

Gabès *Tunisia* 42D1
Gabon 42E4/5
Gaborone *Botswana* 44C3
Gainsborough *England* 20G4
Gairloch *Scotland* 22C3
Galashiels *Scotland* 22F5
Galati *Romania* 29F3
Galicia *Region Spain* 25A1
Galle *Sri Lanka* 39G5
Gallipoli *Italy* 27D2
Gällivare *Sweden* 30E2
Galveston *USA* 7D3
Galway *Ireland* 23B2
Gambia 42B3
Gambier Is. *Pacific Ocean* 47
Gamboma *Congo* 42E5
Gandia *Spain* 25B2
Ganzhou *China* 35F4
Gao *Mali* 42C3
Garve *Scotland* 22D3
Gascogne *Province France* 24B3
Gateshead *England* 20F3
Gauhati *India* 39H3
Gävle *Sweden* 30D3
Gaziantep *Turkey* 38B2
Gdansk *Poland* 29D2
Gdynia *Poland* 29D2
Gedaref *Sudan* 43G3
Geelong *Australia* 45D4
Gejiu *China* 34E4
Gela *Italy* 26C3
General Santos *Philippines* 37E3
Geneva *see* Genève 24D2
Genève (Geneva) *Switzerland* 24D2
Genoa *see* Genova 26B2
Genova (Genoa) *Italy* 26B2
Gent *Belgium* 24C1
George Town *Malaysia* 36C3
Georgetown *Guyana* 16D2
Georgia 32F5
Georgia *State USA* 7E2
Gera *Germany* 28C2
Geraldton *Australia* 45A3
Gerona *Spain* 25C1
Getafe *Spain* 25B1
Gevgelija *Macedonia** 27E2
Ghadamis *Libya* 42D1
Ghana 42C4
Ghat *Libya* 42E2
Gibraltar *Colony SW Europe* 25A2
Gifu *Japan* 35M9
Giglio I. *Italy* 26C2
Gijón *Spain* 25A1
Gilbert Is. *Kiribati* 46
Gilgit *Pakistan* 39F2
Girvan *Scotland* 22D5
Gisborne *New Zealand* 45G4
Giurgiu *Romania* 27F2
Glasgow *Scotland* 22D5
Glenrothes *Scotland* 22E4
Gliwice *Poland* 29D2
Gloucester *England* 21E6
Gniezno *Poland* 28D2
Gobabis *Namibia* 44B3
Godthåb (Nuuk) *Greenland* 5N3
Goiânia *Brazil* 16E4
Goiás *State Brazil* 16E4
Gol *Norway* 30B3
Golmund *China* 34D3
Gomel' *Belarus* 32E4
Gomera *Canary Islands* 42B2
Gonaïves *Haiti* 14E3
Gonder *Ethiopia* 43G3
Goole *England* 20G4
Gorontalo *Indonesia* 37E3
Gort *Ireland* 23C3
Gorzów Wielkopolski *Poland* 28D2
Gospic *Croatia* 26D2
Göteborg *Sweden* 30C4
Gotland I. *Sweden* 30D4
Göttingen *Germany* 28B2
Goulburn *Australia* 45D4
Gran Canaria *Canary Islands* 42B2
Granada *Nicaragua* 14B4
Granada *Spain* 25B2
Grand Bahama I. *The Bahamas* 14D1
Grandola *Portugal* 25A2
Grand Rapids *USA* 7E1
Graz *Austria* 28D3
Great Abaco I. *The Bahamas* 14D1
Greater Antilles Is. *Caribbean Sea* 14C2/D3
Great Exuma I. *The Bahamas* 14D2
Great Inagua I. *The Bahamas* 14E2
Great Nicobar I. *India* 39H5
Great Yarmouth *England* 21J5
Greece 27E2/3
Greenland *Atlantic Ocean* 5O2
Greenock *Scotland* 22D5
Greensboro *USA* 7F2
Grenada, I. *Caribbean* 14G4
Grenadines Is. The *Caribbean Sea* 14G4
Grenoble *France* 24D2
Gretna *Scotland* 22E5
Grimsby *England* 20G4
Grong *Norway* 30C3
Groningen *Netherlands* 28B2
Groote Eylandt I. *Australia* 45C2
Grootfontein *Namibia* 44B2
Grosseto *Italy* 26C2
Groznyy *Russia* 32F5
Grudziadz *Poland* 29D2
Guadalajara *Mexico* 6C3
Guadalajara *Spain* 25B1
Guadalcanal I. *Solomon Islands* 45E2
Guadalupe I. *Mexico* 6B3
Guadeloupe I. *Caribbean Sea* 14G3
Guam *Pacific Ocean* 37G2
Guangdong *Province China* 35F4
Guangxi *Province China* 34E4
Guangzhou *China* 35F4
Guantánamo *Cuba* 14D2
Guarda *Portugal* 25A1
Guatemala *Guatemala* 14A4
Guayaquil *Ecuador* 16B3
Guernsey I. *UK* 21E8
Guiana (French) 16D2
Guildford *England* 21G6
Guilin *China* 35F4
Guinea 42B3
Guinea Bissau 42B3
Güiria *Venezuela* 16C1
Guiyang *China* 34E4
Guizhou *Province China* 34E4
Gulu *Uganda* 43G4
Gur'yev *Kazakhstan* 32G5
Guyana 16D2
Guyenne *Province France* 24B/C3
Gwalior *India* 39F3
Gweru *Zimbabwe* 44C2
Gyandzha *Azerbaijan* 32F5
Györ *Hungary* 29D3H
Haarlem *Netherlands* 28A2
Hachinohe *Japan* 35P6
Hagen *Germany* 28B2
Haifa *Israel* 38B2
Haikou *China* 35F4
Ha'il *Saudi Arabia* 38C3
Hailar *China* 35F2
Hainan Dao I. *China* 35F5
Haiphong *Vietnam* 36C1
Haiti 14E3
Hakodate *Japan* 35J2
Halab *Syria* 38B2
Halden *Norway* 30C4
Halifax *Canada* 5M5
Halifax *England* 20F4
Halle *Germany* 28C2
Halmahera I. *Indonesia* 37E3
Halmstad *Sweden* 30C4
Hamadan *Iran* 38C2
Hamamatsu *Japan* 35M9
Hamar *Norway* 30C3
Hamburg *Germany* 28C2
Hamhung *North Korea* 35G2
Hami *China* 34D2
Hamilton *Canada* 5K5
Hamilton *New Zealand* 45G4
Hamm *Germany* 28B2
Hammerfest *Norway* 30E1
Hanamaki *Japan* 35P7
Handan *China* 35F3
Hangzhou *China* 35G3
Hannover *Germany* 28B2
Hanoi *Vietnam* 36C1
Hanzhong *China* 34E3
Haora *India* 39G3
Harare *Zimbabwe* 44D2
Harbin *China* 35G2
Harer *Ethiopia* 43H4
Hargeysa *Somalia* 43H4
Harlow *England* 21H6
Harris I. *Scotland* 22B3
Harrisburg *USA* 7F1
Harrogate *England* 20F4
Hartford *USA* 7F1
Hartlepool *England* 20F3
Harwich *England* 21J6
Hässleholm *Sweden* 30C4
Hastings *England* 21H7
Hastings *New Zealand* 45G4
Haugesund *Norway* 30B4
Havana *Cuba* 14C2
Havant *England* 21G7
Hawaii *State USA* 6H
Hawaiian Is. *Pacific Ocean* 6H
Hawick *Scotland* 22F5
Hay River *Canada* 5G3
Heanor *England* 20F4
Heard Is. *Indian Ocean* 46
Hebei *Province China* 35F3
Hefei *China* 35F3
Hegang *China* 35H2
Heidelberg *Germany* 28B3
Heilongjiang *Province China* 35G2
Helena *USA* 6B1
Hella *Iceland* 30A2
Hellín *Spain* 25B2
Helmsdale *Scotland* 22E2
Helsinborg *Sweden* 30C4
Helsingfors (Helsinki) *Finland* 30E3
Henan *Province China* 35F3
Hengyang *China* 35F4
Henzada *Myanmar* 36B2
Herat *Afghanistan* 38E2
Hereford *England* 21E5
Hermosillo *USA* 6B3
Hexham *England* 20E3
Hierro *Canary Islands* 42B2
Hiiumaa I. *Estonia* 30E4
Himeji *Japan* 35L9
Hims *Syria* 38B2
Hinckley *England* 21F5
Hinnöy I. *Norway* 30D2
Hiroshima *Japan* 35H3
Hîrsova *Romania* 27F2
Hispaniola I. *Caribbean Sea* 14E3
Hitachi *Japan* 35P8
Hobart *Tasmania* 45D5
Ho Chi Minh City *Vietnam* 36C2
Höfn *Iceland* 30B2
Hohhot *China* 35F2
Hokitika *New Zealand* 45G5
Hokkaido I. *Japan* 35J2
Holguín *Cuba* 14D2

Holy I. *England* 20F2
Holyhead *Wales* 20C4
Honduras 14B4
Hong Kong 35F5
Honiara *Solomon Islands* 45E1
Honolulu *Hawaii, USA* 6H
Horsham *England* 21G6
Hotan *China* 34C3
Hoting *Sweden* 30D3
Houghton-le-Spring *England* 20F3
Houston *USA* 7D3
Hovd *Mongolia* 34D2
Hoy I. *Scotland* 22E2
Hradec-Králové *Czech Republic* 28D2
Huainan *China* 35F3
Huambo *Angola* 44B2
Huancayo *Peru* 16B4
Huangshi *China* 35F3
Hubei *Province China* 35F3
Hubli *India* 39F4
Huddersfield *England* 20F4
Hudiksvall *Sweden* 30D3
Hué *Vietnam* 36C2
Huelva *Spain* 25A2
Hughenden *Australia* 45D3
Humaitá *Brazil* 16C3
Hunan *Province China* 35F4
Hungary 29D/E3
Hunstanton *England* 21H5
Huntly *Scotland* 22F3
Huntsville *USA* 7E2
Húsavik *Iceland* 30B1
Hvar I. *Croatia* 26D2
Hwange *Zimbabwe* 44C2
Hyderabad *India* 39F4
Hyderabad *Pakistan* 39E3
Hythe *England* 21J6

I

Ibadan *Nigeria* 42D4
Ibiza I. *Spain* 25C2
Ibiza *Spain* 25C2
Ica *Peru* 16B4
Iceland *Atlantic Ocean* 5R3
Idaho *State USA* 6B1
Idhra I. *Greece* 27E3
Igarka *Russia* 32K3
Igoumenítsa *Greece* 27E3
Ikaría I. *Greece* 27F3
Ile d'Olêron *France* 24B2
Ile de Noirmoutier *France* 24B2
Ile de Ré *France* 24B2
Ilebo *Dem. Rep. of Congo* 43F5
Iles d'Hyères *France* 24D3
Ilfracombe *England* 21C6
Iliodhrómia I. *Greece* 27E3
Illinois *State USA* 7E1
Iloilo *Philippines* 37E2
Ilorin *Nigeria* 42D4
Imperatriz *Brazil* 16E3
Impfondo *Congo* 43E4
Imphal *India* 39H3
India 39F3/4
Indiana *State USA* 7E1
Indianapolis *USA* 7E2
Indonesia 36/37
Indore *India* 39F3
Inhambane *Mozambique* 44D3
Inner Hebrides *Scotland* 22B4
Inner Mongolia *Province China* 35F2
Innsbruck *Austria* 28C3
In Salah *Algeria* 42D2
Inuvik *Canada* 5E3
Inveraray *Scotland* 22C4
Invercargill *New Zealand* 45F5
Inverness *Scotland* 22D3
Inverurie *Scotland* 22F3
Ioannina *Greece* 27E3
Ios I. *Greece* 27F3
Iowa *State USA* 7D1
Ipoh *Malaysia* 36C3
Ipswich 21J5
Iquique *Chile* 16B5
Iquitos *Peru* 16B3
Iráklion *Greece* 27F3
Iran 38D2
Iraq 38C2
Ireland 23
Iringa *Tanzania* 44D1
Irkutsk *Russia* 33M4
Irvine *Scotland* 22D5
Isafjördhur *Iceland* 30A1
Ischia I. *Italy* 26C2
Ise *Japan* 35M9
Ishinomaki *Japan* 35P7
Isiro *Dem. Rep. of Congo* 43F4
Isla Blanquilla I. *Venezuela* 14G4
Isla Coiba *Panama* 14C5
Isla de Chiloé I. *Chile* 17B7
Isla de la Bahía *Honduras* 14B3
Isla de la Juventud *Cuba* 14C2
Isla del Rey *Panama* 14D5
Isla Los Rogues I. *Venezuela* 14F4
Islamabad *Pakistan* 39F2
Isla Margarita I. *Venezuela* 14G4
Isla Santa Inés I. *Chile* 17B8
Islas Baleares (Balearic Is) *Spain* 25C2
Islas Canarias (Canary Is) *Spain* 42B2
Islay I. *Scotland* 22B5
Isle of Man *UK* 20C3
Isle of Wight *England* 21F7
Isles of Scilly *England* 21A8
Israel 40C2
Istanbul *Turkey* 38A1
Isthmus of Kra *Thailand* 36B3
Itabuna *Brazil* 16F4
Itaituba *Brazil* 16D3
Italy 26C/D2
Iturup I. *Russsian Fed.* 35J2
Ivalo *Finland* 30F2
Ivangrad *Yugoslavia* 26D2
Ivanovo *Russia* 32F4
Iwaki *Japan* 35P8
Iwo Jima *Japan* 37G1
Izhevsk *Russia* 32G4
Izmir *Turkey* 38A2

J

Jabalpur *India* 39F3
Jackson *USA* 7D2
Jacksonville *USA* 7E2
Jacmel *Haiti* 14E3
Jaén *Spain* 25B2
Jaffna *Sri Lanka* 39G5
Jaipur *India* 39F3
Jajce *Bosnia Herzegovina* 26D2
Jakarta *Indonesia* 36C4
Jalgaon *India* 39F3
Jamaica *Caribbean* 14D3
Jambi *Indonesia* 36C4
Jammu *India* 39F2
Jamnagar *India* 39E3
Jämsänkoski *Finland* 30F3
Jamshedpur *India* 39G3
Japan 35H3
Jardines de la Reina *Cuba* 14D2
Jarvis I. *Pacific Ocean* 47
Jawa I. *Indonesia* 36C/D4
Jayapura *Indonesia* 37G4
Jedburgh *Scotland* 22F5
Jedda *see* Jiddah 38B3
Jefferson City *USA* 7D2
Jelenia Góra *Poland* 28D2
Jena *Germany* 28C2
Jequié *Brazil* 16E4
Jerez de la Frontera *Spain* 25A2
Jersey I. *UK* 21E8
Jerusalem *Israel* 38B2
Jhansi *India* 39F3
Jiamusi *China* 35H2
Ji'an *China* 35F4
Jiangsu *Province China* 35F/G3
Jiangxi *Province China* 35F4
Jiddah (Jedda) *Saudi Arabia* 38B3
Jihlava *Czech Republic* 28D3
Jilin *China* 35G2
Jilin *Province China* 35G2
Jima *Ethiopia* 43G4
Jinan *China* 35F3
Jingdezhen *China* 35F4
Jinhua *China* 35F4
Jining *China* 35F3
Jinja *Uganda* 43G4
Jinzhou *China* 35G2
Jiujiang *China* 35F4
João Pessoa *Brazil* 16F3
Jodhpur *India* 39F3
Johannesburg *South Africa* 44C3
John O'Groats *Scotland* 22E2
Johnson I. *Pacific Ocean* 46
Johor Baharu *Malaysia* 36C3
Jokkmokk *Sweden* 30D2
Jolo I. *Philippines* 37E3
Jönköping *Sweden* 30C4
Jordan 38B2
Jörn *Sweden* 30E2
Jos *Nigeria* 42D4
Jotunheimen *Norway* 30B3
Juàzeiro *Brazil* 16E3
Juba *Sudan* 43G4
Jujuy *State Argentina* 17C5
Julianehåb *Greenland* 5O3
Juneau *USA* 6J
Jura I. *Scotland* 22C5
Jutland *see* Jylland 30B4
Jylland (Jutland). *Denmark* 30B4
Jyväskylä *Finland* 30F3

K

Kabul *Afghanistan* 39E2
Kaduna *Nigeria* 42D3
Kaédi *Mauritania* 42B3
Kaesong *North Korea* 35G3
Kagoshima *Japan* 35H3
Kaifeng *China* 35F3
Kailua *Hawaii USA* 6H
Kairouan *Tunisia* 42D1
Kajaani *Finland* 30F3
Kakinada *India* 39G4
Kalabáka *Greece* 27E3
Kalajoki *Finland* 30E3
Kalámai *Greece* 27E3
Kalaupapa *Hawaii USA* 6H
Kalémié *Dem. Rep. of Congo* 43F5
Kalgoorlie *Australia* 45B4
Kálimnos I. *Greece* 27F3
Kaliningrad *Russia* 32D4
Kalisz *Poland* 29D2
Kalmar *Sweden* 30D4
Kamaishi *Japan* 35P7
Kamina *Dem. Rep. of Congo* 44C1
Kamloops *Canada* 5F4
Kampala *Uganda* 43G4
Kananga *Dem. Rep. of Congo* 43F5
Kanazawa *Japan* 35M8
Kandahar *Afghanistan* 39E2
Kandalaksha *Russia* 32E3
Kandangan *Indonesia* 36D4
Kandy *Sri Lanka* 39G5
Kaneohe *Hawaii USA* 6H
Kangaroo I. *Australia* 45C4
Kankan *Guinea* 42C3
Kano *Nigeria* 42D3
Kanpur *India* 39G3
Kansas City *USA* 7D2
Kansas *State USA* 6D2
Kao-hsiung *Taiwan* 37E1
Kaolack *Senegal* 42B3
Karachi *Pakistan* 39E3
Karaganda *Kazakstan* 32J5
Karbala *Iraq* 38C2
Karcag *Hungary* 29E3
Karlobag *Croatia* 26D2
Karlovac *Croatia* 26D1
Karlshamn *Sweden* 30C4
Karlskoga *Sweden* 30C4
Karlskrona *Sweden* 30D4
Karlsruhe *Germany* 28B3
Karlstad *Sweden* 30C4
Kárpathos I. *Greece* 27F3
Karshi *Uzbekistan* 32H6
Kasama *Zimbabwe* 44D2
Kasese *Uganda* 43G4
Kashi *China* 34B3
Kásos I. *Greece* 27F3
Kassala *Sudan* 43G3
Kassel *Germany* 28B2
Kastoria *Greece* 27E2
Kateríni *Greece* 27E2
Katherine *Australia* 45C2
Kathmandu *Nepal* 39G3
Katowice *Poland* 29D2
Katsina *Nigeria* 42D3
Kauai I. *Hawaii USA* 6H
Kaunas *Lithuania* 30E5
Kaválla *Greece* 27E2
Kawaihae *Hawaii USA* 6H
Kawasaki *Japan* 35N9
Kayes *Mali* 42B3
Kayseri *Turkey* 38B2
Kazakhstan 32H/J5
Kazan *Russia* 32F4
Kazanlük *Bulgaria* 27F2
Kazan-rettó *Japan* 37G1
Kéa I. *Greece* 27E3
Kecskemét *Hungary* 29D3
Kediri *Indonesia* 36D4
Keetmanshoop *Namibia* 44B3
Kefallnía I. *Greece* 27E3
Keflavik *Iceland* 30A2
Keighley *England* 20F4
Keith *Scotland* 22F3
Kelang *Malaysia* 36C3
Kells *Ireland* 23E3
Kemerovo *Russia* 32K4
Kemi *Finland* 30E2
Kemijärvi *Finland* 30F2
Kendal *England* 20E3
Kendari *Indonesia* 37E4
Kengtung *Myanmar* 36B1
Kenitra *Morocco* 42C1
Kenmare *Ireland* 23B5
Kenora *Canada* 5J5
Kentucky *State USA* 7E2
Kenya 43G4/5
Kep. Anambas I. *Indonesia* 36C3
Kep. Aru I. *Indonesia* 37F4
Kep. Banggai I. *Indonesia* 37E4
Kep. Kai I. *Indonesia* 37F4
Kep. Leti I. *Indonesia* 37E4
Kep. Mentawai, Arch. *Indonesia* 36B4
Kepno *Poland* 29D2
Kep. Sangihe I. *Indonesia* 37E3
Kep. Sula I. *Indonesia* 37E4
Kep. Talaud I. *Indonesia* 37E3
Kep. Togian I. *Indonesia* 37E4
Kepulauan Tanimbar I. *Indonesia* 37F4
Kerch *Ukraine* 32E5
Kerguelen Is. *Indian Ocean* 46
Kérkira *Greece* 27D3
Kermadec Is. *Pacific Ocean* 46
Kerman *Iran* 38D2
Keswick *England* 20E3
Key West *USA* 7E3
Khabarovsk *Russia* 33P5
Khalkis *Greece* 27E3
Khaniá *Greece* 27E3
Khar'kov *Ukraine* 32E4
Kharagpur *India* 39G3
Khartoum *Sudan* 43G3
Khartoum North *Sudan* 43G3
Khíos I. *Greece* 27F3
Khulna *Bangladesh* 39G3
Kiel *Germany* 28C2
Kielce *Poland* 29E2
Kiev *see* Kiyev 32E4
Kigali *Rwanda* 43G5
Kigoma *Tanzania* 43F5
Kikladhes Is. *Greece* 27E/F3
Kikwit *Dem. Rep. of Congo* 43E5
Kildare *Ireland* 23E3
Kilkenny *Ireland* 23D4
Killarney *Ireland* 23B4
Kilmarnock *Scotland* 22D5
Kilrush *Ireland* 23B4
Kimberley *South Africa* 44C3
Kindia *Guinea* 42B3
Kindu *Dem. Rep. of Congo* 43F5
King I. *Australia* 45D4
Kings Lynn *England* 21H5
Kingston *Jamaica* 14D3
Kingston-upon-Hull *England* 20G4
Kingstown *St Vincent* 14G4
Kingswood *England* 21E6
Kingussie *Scotland* 22D3
Kinnegad *Ireland* 23D3
Kintyre I. *Scotland* 22C5
Kinvarra *Ireland* 23C3
Kiribati Is. *Pacific Ocean* 46
Kiritimati *Kiribati* 47
Kirkby Stephen *England* 20E3
Kirkcaldy *Scotland* 22E4
Kirkenes *Norway* 30G2
Kirkuk *Iraq* 38C2
Kirkwall *Scotland* 22F2
Kirov *Russia* 32F4
Kiruna *Sweden* 30E2
Kisangani *Dem. Rep. of Congo* 43F4
Kishinev *Moldova* 32D5
Kiskunfélegyháza *Hungary* 29D3
Kismaayo *Somalia* 43H5
Kisumu *Kenya* 43G5
Kita-Kyushu *Japan* 35H3
Kithira I. *Greece* 27E3
Kíthnos I. *Greece* 27E3
Kitwe *Zambia* 44C2
Kiyev (Kiev) *Ukraine* 32E4
Kladno *Czech Republic* 28C2
Klagenfurt *Austria* 28C3
Klaipeda *Lithuania* 32D4
Klerksdorp *South Africa* 44C3
Knoxville *USA* 7E2
Kobe *Japan* 35L9
København (Copenhagen) *Denmark* 30C4
Koblenz *Germany* 28B2
Kochi *Japan* 35H3
Kodiak I. *USA* 6J
Kofu *Japan* 35N9
Kokkola *Finland* 30E3
Kolding *Denmark* 30B4
Kolhapur *India* 39F4
Köln (Cologne) *Germany* 28B2
Koloma *Russia* 32E4
Kolwezi *Dem. Rep. of Congo* 44C2
Komatsu *Japan* 35M8
Komotiní *Greece* 27F2
Kompong Cham *Cambodia* 36C2
Kompong Som *Cambodia* 36C2
Komsomol'sk na-Amure *Russia* 33P4
Konin *Poland* 29D2
Konjic *Bosnia Herzegovina* 27D2
Konya *Turkey* 38B2
Kópavogur *Iceland* 30A2
Korcë *Albania* 27E2
Korcula I. *Croatia* 26D2
Korea, *North* 35G2/3
Korea, *South* 35G3
Kórinthos (Corinth) *Greece* 27E3
Koriyama *Japan* 35P8
Kornat I. *Croatia* 26D2
Korsör *Denmark* 30C4
Kós I. *Greece* 27F3
Kosice *Slovakia* 29E3
Kosovo *Region Yugoslavia* 27E2
Kosovska-Mitrovica *Yugoslavia* 27E2
Koszalin *Poland* 28D2
Kota *India* 39F3
Kota Baharu *Malaysia* 36C3
Kota Kinabalu *Malaysia* 36D3
Kotka *Finland* 30F3
Kotlas *Russia* 32F3
Kotor *Yugoslavia* 27D2
Kouvola *Finland* 30F3
Kowloon *Hong Kong* 36D1
Kragujevac *Yugoslavia* 27E2
Kraków *Poland* 29D2
Kramsfors *Sweden* 30D3
Kranj *Slovenia* 26C1
Krasnodar *Russia* 32E5
Krasnovodsk *Turkmenistan* 32G5
Krasnoyarsk *Russia* 33L4
Krefeld *Germany* 28B2
Kristiansand *Norway* 30B4
Kristianstad *Sweden* 30C4
Krivoy Rog *Ukraine* 32E5
Krk I. *Croatia* 26C1
Kruscevac *Yugoslavia* 27E2
Kuala Lumpur *Malaysia* 36C3
Kuala Terengganu *Malaysia* 36C3
Kuching *Malaysia* 36D3
Kulata *Bulgaria* 27E2
Kumamoto *Japan* 35H3
Kumanovo **Macedonia* 27E2
Kumasi *Ghana* 42C4
Kunashir I. *Russia* 35J2
Kunming *China* 34E4
Kuopio *Finland* 30F3
Kupang *Indonesia* 37E5
Kuril'Skiye Ostrova *Russia* 33Q/R5
Kurnool *India* 39F4
Kursk *Russia* 32E4
Kushiro *Japan* 35J2
Kuwait 38C3
Kwangju *South Korea* 35G3
Kyle of Lochalsh *Scotland* 22C3
Kyoto *Japan* 35L9
Kyrgyzstan 32J5
Kyzyl *Russia* 33L4
Kzyl Orda *Kazakhstan* 32H5

L

Laâyoune *Western Sahara* 42B2
Labé *Guinea* 42B3
Lábrea *Brazil* 16C3
Labytnangi *Russia* 32H3
La Ceiba *Honduras* 14B4
La Coruña *Spain* 25A1
Lae *Papua New Guinea* 39G4
La Flèche *France* 24B2
Lagos *Nigeria* 42D4
Lagos *Portugal* 25A2
La Habana *Cuba* 14C2
Lahore *Pakistan* 39F2
Lahti *Finland* 30F3
Lai Chau *Vietnam* 36C1
Lairg *Scotland* 22D2
Lajes *Brazil* 17D5
Lakshadweep Is. *India* 39F4
Lambaréné *Gabon* 42E5
Lamía *Greece* 27E3
Lampang *Thailand* 36B2
Lampedusa I. *Italy* 26C3
Lampione I. *Italy* 26C3
Lanai I. *Hawaii USA* 6H
Lanark *Scotland* 22E5
Lancaster *England* 20E3
Lang Son *Vietnam* 36C1
Langres *France* 24D2
Languedoc *Province France* 24C3
Lansing *USA* 7E1
Lanzarote I. *Canary Islands* 42B2
Lanzhou *China* 34E3
Laoag *Philippines* 37E2
Lao Cai *Vietnam* 36C1
Laos 36C2
La Palma *Canary Islands* 42B2
La Pampa *State Argentina* 17C6
La Paz *Bolivia* 16C4
La Plata *Argentina* 17D6
L'Aquila *Italy* 26C2
Laredo *USA* 6D3
Largs *Scotland* 22D5
La Rioja *Region Spain* 25B1
La Rioja *State Argentina* 16C5
Lárisa *Greece* 27E3
Larne *Northern Ireland* 23F2
La Rochelle *France* 24B2
La Roda *Spain* 25B2
La Romana *Dominican Republic* 14F3
La Serena *Chile* 17B5
Lashio *Myanmar* 36B1
Las Palmas de Gran Canaria *Canary Islands* 42B2
La Spezia *Italy* 26B2
Lastovo I. *Croatia* 26D2

Las Vegas *USA* 6B2
Latina *Italy* 26C2
La Tortuga I. *Venezuela* 14F4
Latvia 30E4
Launceston *Tasmania* 45D5
Laurencekirk *Scotland* 22F4
Lausanne *Switzerland* 24D2
Laut I. *Indonesia* 36D4
Laval *France* 24B2
Lebanon 40C1
Leeds *England* 20F4
Leeuwarden *Netherlands* 28B2
Leeward Is. *Caribbean Sea* 14G3
Legazpi *Philippines* 37E2
Le Havre *France* 24C2
Leicester *England* 21F5
Leipzig *Germany* 28C2
Leiria *Portugal* 25A2
Le Mans *France* 24C2
Lens *France* 24C1
León *Mexico* 6C3
León *Nicaragua* 14B4
León *Spain* 25A1
Lérida *Spain* 25C1
Léros I. *Greece* 27F3
Lerwick *Scotland* 22J7
Les Cayes *Haiti* 14E3
Leshan *China* 34E4
Leskovac *Yugoslavia* 27E2
Lesotho 44C3
Lesser Antilles Is. *Caribbean* 14F4
Lésvós I. *Greece* 27F3
Letterkenny *Ireland* 23D2
Levkás I. *Greece* 27E3
Lewes *England* 21H7
Lewis I. *Scotland* 22B2
Leyte I. *Philippines* 37E2
Lhasa *China* 39H3
Lhasa *China* 34D4
Lianoyang *China* 35G2
Lianyungang *China* 35F3
Liaoning *Province China* 35G3
Liaoyuan *China* 35G2
Liberec *Czech Republic* 28D2
Liberia 42B4
Libreville *Gabon* 42D4
Libya 42E2
Lichinga *Mozambique* 44D2
Liechtenstein 28B3
Liège *Belgium* 24D1
Liepaja *Latvia* 30E4
Likasi *Dem. Rep. of Congo* 44C2
Lille *France* 24C1
Lillehammer *Norway* 30C3
Lilongwe *Malawi* 44D2
Lima *Peru* 16B4
Limerick *Ireland* 23C4
Límnos *Greece* 27F3
Limoges *France* 24C2
Limón *Costa Rica* 14C5
Limousin *Province France* 24C2
Linares *Spain* 25B2
Lincang *China* 34E4
Lincoln *England* 20G4
Lincoln *USA* 6D1
Linfen *China* 35F3
Linköping *Sweden* 30D4
Linosa I. *Italy* 26C3
Linz *Austria* 28C3
Lipari I. *Italy* 26C3
Lisboa (Lisbon) *Portugal* 25A2
Lisbon see Lisboa 25A2
Lisburn *Northern Ireland* 23E2
Lisieux *France* 24C2
Lithuania 30E4
Little Rock *USA* 7D2
Liuzhou *China* 34E4
Livanátais *Greece* 27E3
Liverpool *England* 20E4
Livingston *Scotland* 22E5
Livingstone *Zambia* 44C2
Livno *Bosnia Herzegovina* 26D2
Livorno *Italy* 26C2
Ljubljana *Slovenia* 26C1
Llandrindod Wells *Wales* 21D5
Lobito *Angola* 44B2
Lochboisdale *Scotland* 22A3
Lochgilphead *Scotland* 22C4
Lochinver *Scotland* 22C2
Lochmaddy *Scotland* 22A3
Locri *Italy* 26D3
Lódz *Poland* 29D2
Logroño *Spain* 25B1
Loja *Ecuador* 16B3
Loja *Spain* 25B2
Lolland I. *Denmark* 30C5
Lom *Bulgaria* 27E2
Lombok I. *Indonesia* 36D4
Lome *Togo* 42D4
London *England* 21G6
Londonderry *Northern Ireland* 23D1
Long Island I. *USA* 7F1
Long Island *The Bahamas* 14E2
Longford *Ireland* 23D3
Lorca *Spain* 25B2
Lord Howe I. *Australia* 45F4
Lorient *France* 24B2
Los Angeles *USA* 6B2
Los Mochis *Mexico* 6C3
Losinj I. *Croatia* 26C2
Louisiana *State USA* 7D2
Louisville *USA* 7E2
Loukhi *Russia* 30G2
Louth *England* 20G4
Loznica *Yugoslavia* 27D2
Lu'an *China* 35F3
Luanda *Angola* 44B1
Luang Prabang *Laos* 36C2
Lubango *Angola* 44B2
Lubbock *USA* 6C2
Lübeck *Germany* 28C2
Lublin *Poland* 29E2
Lubumbashi *Dem. Rep. of Congo* 44C2
Lucca *Italy* 26C2
Lucknow *India* 39G3
Lüda *China* 35G3
Lüderitz *Namibia* 44B3
Ludhiana *India* 39F2
Ludvika *Sweden* 30D3
Luga *Russia* 30F4
Lugansk *Russia* 32E5
Lugo *Spain* 25A1
Luleå *Sweden* 30E2
Lundy I. *England* 21C6
Luohe *China* 35F3
Luoyang *China* 35F3
Lurgan *Northern Ireland* 23E2
Lusaka *Zambia* 44C2
Luton *England* 21G6
Luxembourg *Luxembourg* 24D2
Luxor *Egypt* 43G2
Luzern *Switzerland* 24D2
Luzern *Switzerland* 26B1
Luzhou *China* 34E4
Luzon I. *Philippines* 37E2
L'vov *Ukraine* 32D5
Lybster *Scotland* 22E2
Lycksele *Sweden* 30D3
Lyon *France* 24C2

M

Maastricht *Netherlands* 28B2
Ma'an *Jordan* 38B2
Macapá *Brazil* 16D2
Macau *Hong Kong* 36D1
Macclesfield *England* 20E4
Maceió *Brazil* 16F3
Macedonia Republic 27E2
Mackay *Australia* 45D3
Macomer *Italy* 26B2
Mâcon *France* 24C2
Macon *USA* 7E2
Macquarie I. *New Zealand* 46
Madagascar 44E3
Madang *Papua New Guinea* 37G4
Madeira I. *Atlantic Ocean* 42B1
Madison *USA* 7E1
Madras *India* 39G4
Madrid *Spain* 25B1
Madura I. *Indonesia* 36D4
Madurai *India* 39F5
Mafia I. *Tanzania* 44D1
Mafikeng *South Africa* 44C3
Magadan *Russia* 33R4
Magdeburg *Germany* 28C2
Magnitogorsk *Russia* 32G4
Mahajanga *Madagascar* 44E2
Mahalapye *Botswana* 44C3
Mahón *Spain* 25C2
Maidstone *England* 21H6
Maiduguri *Nigeria* 42E3
Maine *Province France* 24B2
Maine *State USA* 7F/G1
Mainland I. *Orkney Islands Scotland* 22J7
Mainland I. *Shetland Islands Scotland* 22E1
Mainz *Germany* 28B3
Maitland *Australia* 45E4
Maizuru *Japan* 35L9
Majene *Indonesia* 36D4
Majorca I. *Spain* 25C2
Makarska *Croatia* 26D2
Makhachkala *Russia* 32F5
Makkah *Saudi Arabia* 38B3
Makó *Hungary* 29E3
Makurdi *Nigeria* 42D4
Malabo *Bioko Islands* 42D4
Malaga *Spain* 25B2
Malakal *Sudan* 43G4
Malang *Indonesia* 36D4
Malanje *Angola* 44B1
Malawi 44D2
Malatya *Turkey* 38B2
Malaysia 36C3
Malden I. *Kiribati* 47
Maldives Is. *Indian Ocean* 39F5
Malekula I. *Vanuatu* 45F2
Mali 42C3
Mallaig *Scotland* 22C3
Mallow *Ireland* 23C4
Malmö *Sweden* 30C4
Malta 26C3
Malton *England* 20G3
Mamou *Guinea* 42B3
Man *Côte d'Ivoire* 42C4
Mana *Hawaii USA* 6H
Manacor *Spain* 25C2
Manado *Indonesia* 37E3
Managua *Nicaragua* 14B4
Manakara *Madagascar* 44E3
Manaus *Brazil* 16C3
Manchester *England* 20E4
Mandal *Norway* 30B4
Mandalay *Myanmar* 36B1
Manfredonia *Italy* 26D2
Mangalia *Romania* 27F2
Mangalore *India* 39F4
Manila *Philippines* 37E2
Manitoba *Province Canada* 5H/J4
Manizales *Colombia* 16B2
Mannheim *Germany* 28B3
Manokwari *Indonesia* 37F4
Mansfield *England* 20F4
Manta *Ecuador* 16A3
Mantes *France* 24C2
Manzanares *Spain* 25B2
Manzanillo *Cuba* 14D2
Manzhouli *China* 35F2
Maoming *China* 35F4
Maputo *Mozambique* 44D3
Maracaibo *Venezuela* 16B1
Maradi *Niger* 42D3
Maranhão *State Brazil* 16E3
Marbella *Spain* 25B2
Marburg *Germany* 28B2
Mardan *Pakistan* 39F2
Mar del Plata *Argentina* 17D6
Margate *England* 21J6
Maribor *Slovenia* 26D1
Marie-Galante I. *Caribbean Sea* 14G3
Mariestad *Sweden* 30C4
Marília *Brazil* 16E5
Mariupol *Ukraine* 32E5
Marmaris *Turkey* 27F3
Maroua *Cameroon* 42E3
Marquises Is. *Pacific Ocean* 46
Marrakech *Morocco* 42C1
Marseille *France* 24D3
Marshall Is. *Pacific Ocean* 46
Martinique I. *Caribbean Sea* 14G4
Mary *Turkmenistan* 32H6
Maryland *State USA* 7F2
Masaya *Nicaragua* 14B4
Masbate I. *Philippines* 37E2
Maseru *Lesotho* 44C3
Mashhad *Iran* 38D2
Masīrah I. *Oman* 38D3
Masqat (Muscat) *Oman* 38D3
Massa *Italy* 26C2
Massachusetts *State USA* 7F1
Matadi *Dem. Rep. of Congo* 42E5
Matagalpa *Nicaragua* 14B4
Matamoros *Mexico* 6D3
Matanzas *Cuba* 14C2
Mataram *Indonesia* 36D4
Matlock *England* 20F4
Mato Grosso *State Brazil* 16D4
Mato Grosso do Sul *State Brazil* 16D4/5
Matsue *Japan* 35H3
Matsumoto *Japan* 35M8
Matsusaka *Japan* 35M9
Matsuyama *Japan* 35H3
Maui *Hawaii USA* 6H
Mauritania 42B2
Mauritius I. *Indian Ocean* 44F4
Mayaguana I. *The Bahamas* 14E2
Maybole *Scotland* 22D5
Mayotte I. *Indian Ocean* 44E2
Mazār-e Sharif *Afghanistan* 39E2
Mazatlán *Mexico* 6C3
Mbabane *Swaziland* 44D3
Mbandaka *Dem. Rep. of Congo* 43E4
Mbarara *Uganda* 43G5
Mbeya *Tanzania* 44D1
Mbuji-Mayi *Dem. Rep. of Congo* 43F5
Meaux *France* 24C2
Medan *Indonesia* 36B3
Medellín *Colombia* 16B2
Medgidia *Romania* 27F2
Medicine Hat *Canada* 5G4
Meerut *India* 39F3
Meiktila *Myanmar* 36B1
Meknès *Morocco* 42C1
Melaka *Malaysia* 36C3
Melbourne *Australia* 45D4
Melilla *Spain* 25B2
Melitopol' *Ukraine* 32E5
Melo *Uruguay* 17D6
Melun *France* 24C2
Melvich *Scotland* 22E2
Melville I. *Australia* 45C2
Melville I. *Canada* 5G2
Melville Pen. *Canada* 5K3
Memphis *USA* 7E2
Mende *France* 24C3
Mendoza *Argentina* 17C6
Mendoza *State Argentina* 17C6
Menongue *Angola* 44B2
Merauke *Indonesia* 37G4
Mercedes *Argentina* 17C6
Mergui Arch. *Myanmar* 36B2
Mérida *Mexico* 7E3
Mérida *Spain* 25A2
Merthyr Tydfil *Wales* 21D6
Mesolóngian *Greece* 27E3
Messina *Italy* 26D3
Metz *France* 24D2
Mexicali *USA* 6B2
México *Mexico* 6D4
Meymaneh *Afghanistan* 39E2
Miami *USA* 7E3
Mianyang *China* 34E3
Michigan *State USA* 7E1
Michurin *Bulgaria* 27F2
Middlesbrough *England* 20F3
Midway Is. *Pacific Ocean* 46
Mikkeli *Finland* 30F3
Míkonos I. *Greece* 27F3
Milan *see* Milano 26B1
Milano (Milan) *Italy* 26B1
Mildura *Australia* 45D4
Milford Haven *Wales* 20B6
Millau *France* 24C3
Mílos I. *Greece* 27E3
Milton Keynes *England* 21G5
Milwaukee *USA* 7E1
Minas Gerais *State Brazil* 16E4
Minatinán *Mexico* 7D4
Mindanao *Philippines* 37E3
Mindoro I. *Philippines* 37E2
Minna *Nigeria* 42D4
Minneapolis *USA* 7D1
Minnesota *State USA* 7D1
Minorca I. *Spain* 25C2
Minsk *Belarus* 32D4
Miranda de Ebro *Spain* 25B1
Miri *Malaysia* 36D3
Mirzapur *India* 39G3
Misiones *State Argentina* 17D5
Miskolc *Hungary* 29E3
Misoöl I. *Indonesia* 37F4
Misrātah *Libya* 42E1
Mississippi *State USA* 7D2
Missouri *State USA* 7D2
Mito *Japan* 35P8
Mits'iwa *Ethiopia* 43G3
Miyako *Japan* 35P7
Miyazaki *Japan* 35H3
Mizusawa *Japan* 35P7
Mjölby *Sweden* 30D4
Mlawa *Poland* 29E2
Mljet I. *Croatia* 26D2
Mo-i-Rana *Norway* 30C2
Mobile *USA* 7E2
Moçambique *Mozambique* 44E2
Modena *Italy* 26C2
Moffat *Scotland* 22E5
Mogadishu *Somalia* 43H4
Mogilev *Belarus* 32E4
Mokp'o *South Korea* 35G3
Molde *Norway* 30B3
Moldova (Moldavia) 29F3
Mollendo *Peru* 16B4
Molokai I. *Hawaii USA* 6H
Mombasa *Kenya* 43G5
Monaco *Monaco* 24D3
Monaghan *Ireland* 23E2
Mondovi *Italy* 26B2
Mongolia 33L5
Mongu *Zambia* 44C2
Monopoli *Italy* 27D2
Monreal del Campo *Spain* 25B1
Monrovia *Liberia* 42B4
Montana *State USA* 6B1
Montargis *France* 24C2
Montauban *France* 24C3
Montbéliard *France* 24D2
Monte Cristi *Haiti* 14E3
Montego Bay *Jamaica* 14D3
Montenegro Republic 27D2
Montería *Colombia* 16B2
Monterrey *Mexico* 6C3
Montes Claros *Brazil* 16E4
Montevideo *Uruguay* 17D6
Montgomery *USA* 7E2
Montluçon *France* 24C2
Montpelier *USA* 7F1
Montréal *Canada* 5L5
Montrose *Scotland* 22F4
Montserrat I. *Caribbean Sea* 14G3
Monza *Italy* 26B1
Mopti *Mali* 42C3
Mora *Sweden* 30C3
Moradabad *India* 39F3
Morioka *Japan* 35P7
Morocco 42C1
Moroni *Comoros* 44E2
Morotai I. *Indonesia* 37E3
Morwell *Australia* 45D4
Moscow *see* Moskva 32E4
Moshi *Tanzania* 43G5
Mosjöen *Norway* 30C2
Moskva (Moscow) *Russia* 32E4
Moss *Norway* 30C4
Mossoró *Brazil* 16F3
Mostaganem *Algeria* 42D1
Mostar *Bosnia Herzegovina* 27D2
Motherwell *Scotland* 22E5
Motril *Spain* 25B2
Moulins *France* 24C2
Moulmein *Myanmar* 36B2
Moundou *Chad* 42E4
Mount Gambier *Australia* 45D4
Mount Isa *Australia* 45C3
Mozambique 44D3
Mt. Magnet *Australia* 45A3
Mtwara *Tanzania* 44E2
Muang Nakhon Sawan *Thailand* 36C2
Muand Phitsanulok *Thailand* 36C2
Mudanjiang *China* 35G2
Mufulira *Zambia* 44C2
Muhos *Finland* 30F3
Mulhouse *France* 24D2
Mull I. *Scotland* 22C4
Mullingar *Ireland* 23D3
Multan *Pakistan* 39F2
Muna I. *Indonesia* 37E4
München (Munich) *Germany* 28C3
Mungbere *Dem. Rep. of Congo* 43F4
Münster *Germany* 28B2
Muonio *Finland* 30E2
Muqdisho *see* Mogadishu 43H4
Murcia *Region Spain* 25B2
Murcia *Spain* 25B2
Murmansk *Russia* 32E3
Muscat *see* Masqat 38D3
Musselburgh *Scotland* 22E5
Mutare *Zimbabwe* 44D2
Mwanza *Tanzania* 43G5
Mwene Ditu *Dem. Rep. of Congo* 43F5
Myanmar (Burma) 36B1
Myingyan *Myanmar* 36B1
Myitkyina *Myanmar* 36B1
Mymensingh *Bangladesh* 39H3
Mysore *India* 39F4
My Tho *Vietnam* 36C2

N

Naas *Ireland* 23E3
Naga *Philippines* 37E2
Nagano *Japan* 35N8
Nagaoka *Japan* 35N8
Nagasaki *Japan* 35G3
Nagercoil *India* 39F5
Nagoya *Japan* 35M9
Nagpur *India* 39F3
Nagykanizsa *Hungary* 28D3
Nain *Canada* 5M4
Nairn *Scotland* 22E3
Nairobi *Kenya* 43G5
Nakhodka *Russia* 33P5
Nakhon Ratchasima *Thailand* 36C2
Nakhon Sawan *Thailand* 36C2
Nakhon Si Thammarat *Thailand* 36B3
Nakuru *Kenya* 43G5
Namangan *Kyrgyzstan* 32J5
Nam Dinh *Vietnam* 36C1
Namibe *Angola* 44B2
Namibia 44B3
Nampula *Mozambique* 44D2
Nanchang *China* 35F4
Nanchong *China* 34E3
Nancy *France* 24D2
Nanjing *China* 35F3
Nanning *China* 34E4
Nanping *China* 35F4
Nantes *France* 24B2
Nantong *China* 35G3
Nanyang *China* 35F3
Napoli (Naples) *Italy* 26C2
Narbonne *France* 24C3
Narva *Estonia* 30F4
Narvik *Norway* 30D2
Nar'yan Mar *Russia* 32G3
Nashville *USA* 7E2
Nassau *The Bahamas* 14D1
Natal *Brazil* 16F3
Natuna Besar I. *Indonesia* 36C3
Nauru 46
Navarra *Region Spain* 25B1
Náxos I. *Greece* 27F3

Ndjamena *Chad* 42E3
Ndola *Zambia* 44C2
Neápolis *Greece* 27E3
Near Islands *USA* 6J
Nebraska *State USA* 6C1
Negros I. *Philippines* 37E3
Nei Mongol Zizhiqu *Province China* 35F2
Neiva *Colombia* 16B2
Nellore *India* 39F/G4
Nelson *England* 20E4
Nelson *New Zealand* 45G5
Nenagh *Ireland* 23C4
Nepal 39G3
Netherlands 28A2
Neubrandenburg *Germany* 28C2
Neumünster *Germany* 28B2
Neuquén *Argentina* 17C6
Neuquén *State Argentina* 17C6
Nevada *State USA* 6B2
Nevers *France* 24C2
Newark *USA* 7F1
Newark-on-Trent *England* 20G4
New Britain I. *Pacific Ocean* 37G4
New Brunswick *Canada* 5M5
Newcastle *Australia* 45E4
Newcastle upon Tyne *England* 20F3
New Delhi *India* 39F3
Newfoundland *Province Canada* 5N4
New Georgia *Solomon Islands* 45E1
New Hampshire *State USA* 7F1
New Jersey *State USA* 7F1
New Mexico *State USA* 6C2
New Orleans *USA* 7E3
Newport *Isle of Wight* 21F7
Newport *Wales* 21E6
Newquay *England* 21B7
New Ross *Ireland* 23E4
Newry *Northern Ireland* 23E2
New South Wales *State Australia* 45D4
Newton Aycliffe *England* 20F3
Newton Stewart *Scotland* 22D6
Newtown-Abbey *Northern Ireland* 23F2
New York *State USA* 7F1
New York *USA* 7F1
New Zealand 45G5
Ngaoundére *Cameroon* 42E4
Nguru *Nigeria* 42E3
Nha Trang *Vietnam* 36C2
Niamey *Niger* 42D3
Nias I. *Indonesia* 36B3
Nicaragua 14B4
Nice *France* 24D3
Nicobar I. *India* 39H5
Nicosia *Cyprus* 38B2
Niger 42D3
Nigeria 42D4
Niigata *Japan* 35N8
Nijmegen *Netherlands* 28B2
Nikel *Russia* 30G2
Nikolayev *Ukraine* 32E5
Nîmes *France* 24C3
Ningbo *China* 35G4
Ningxia *Province China* 34E3
Nioro du Sahel *Mali* 42C3
Niort *France* 24B2
Nis *Yugoslavia* 27E2
Nitra *Slovakia* 29D3
Niue I. *Pacific Ocean* 46
Nivernais *Province France* 24C2
Nizamabad *India* 39F4
Nizhniy Tagil *Russia* 32H4
Nizhriy Novgorod *Russia* 32F4
Nkongsamba *Cameroon* 42D4
Nong Khai *Thailand* 36C2
Norfolk I. *Australia* 45F3
Norfolk *USA* 7F2
Noril'sk *Russia* 32K3
Normandie (Normandy) *Province France* 24B2
Norrköping *Sweden* 30D4
Norseman *Australia* 45B4
Northampton 21G5
North Bay *Canada* 5L5
North Carolina *State USA* 7E2
North Dakota *State USA* 6C1
Northern Mariana Is. *Pacific Ocean* 37G2/46
Northern Territory *State Australia* 45C2
North Island *New Zealand* 45G4
North Ronaldsay I. *Scotland* 22F1
North Uist I. *Scotland* 22A3
Northumberland *England* 20E2
Northwest Territories *Canada* 5G3
Norway 30B3
Norwich *England* 21J5
Notodden *Norway* 30B4
Nottingham *England* 21F5
Nouadhibou *Mauritania.* 42B2
Nouakchott *Mauritania.* 42B3
Nouméa *Nouvelle Calédonie* 45F3
Nouvelle Calédonie I. *Pacific Ocean* 45F3
Novara *Italy* 26B1
Nova Scotia *Canada* 5M5
Novaya Zemlya *Russia* 32G2
Novi Pazar *Yugoslavia* 27E2
Novi Sad *Yugoslavia* 27D1
Novokuznatsk *Russia* 32K4
Novorossiysk *Russia* 32E5
Novosibirsk *Russia* 32K4
Novosibirskiye Ostrova I. 33Q2
Nuku'alofa *Tonga* 46
Nukus *Uzbekistan* 32G5
Numazu *Japan* 35N9
Nunivak I. *USA* 5B3
Nürnberg *Germany* 28B3
Nuuk *see* Godthåb 5N3
Nyala *Sudan* 43F3
Nyíregyháza *Hungary* 29E3
Nyköping *Sweden* 30D4
Nyngan *Australia* 45D4
Nzérekoré *Guinea* 42C4

O

Oahu I. *Hawaii USA* 6H
Oban *Scotland* 22C4
Obi I. *Indonesia* 37E4
Odawara *Japan* 35N9
Odda *Norway* 30B3
Odemira *Portugal* 25A2
Odense *Denmark* 30C4
Odessa *USA* 6C2
Odessa *Ukraine* 32D5
Offenbach *Germany* 28B2
Ogaki *Japan* 35M9
Ogasawara-Shotó Is. *Japan* 37G1
Ogbomosho *Nigeria* 42D4
Ogden *USA* 6B1
Ohrid *Macedonia** 27E2
Okaya *Japan* 35N8
Okayama *Japan* 35H3
Okazaki *Japan* 35M9
Okehampton *England* 21C7
Okhotsk *Russia* 33Q4
Okinawa I. *Japan* 35G4
Oklahoma *City USA* 6D2
Oklahoma *State USA* 6D2
Öland I. *Sweden* 30D4
Olbia *Italy* 26B2
Oldenburg *Germany* 28B2
Olomouc *Czech Republic* 28D3
Olsztyn *Poland* 29E2
Olympia *USA* 6A1
Omagh *Northern Ireland* 23D2
Omaha *USA* 6D1
Oman 38D3
Omdurman *Sudan* 43G3
Omsk *Russia* 32J4
Onitsha *Nigeria* 42D4
Ontario *Province Canada* 5J4
Oostende *Belgium* 24C1
Opole *Poland* 29D2
Oppdal *Norway* 30B3
Oradea *Romania* 29E3
Oran *Algeria* 42C1
Orange *Australia* 45D4
Orange *France* 24C3
Orbetello *Italy* 26C2
Orléanais *Province France* 24C2
Örebro *Sweden* 30D4
Oregon *State USA* 6A1
Orel *Russia* 32E4
Orenburg *Russia* 32G4
Orense *Spain* 25A1
Oristano *Italy* 26B3
Orkney Is. *Scotland* 22E1
Orlando *USA* 7E3
Orléans *France* 24C2
Örnsköldsvik *Sweden* 30D3
Orsk *Russia* 32G4
Oruro *Bolivia* 16C4
Osaka *Japan* 35L9
Oshogbo *Nigeria* 42D4
Osijek *Croatia* 27D1
Oskarshamn *Sweden* 30D4
Oslo *Norway* 30C4
Osnabrück *Germany* 28B2
Osorno *Chile* 17B7
Östersund *Sweden* 30C3
Ostia *Italy* 26C2
Ostrava *Czech Republic* 29D3
Osumi-shoto I. *Japan* 35H3
Oswestry *England* 21D5
Otaru *Japan* 35J2
Ottawa *Canada* 5L5
Ouagadougou *Burkina Faso* 42C3
Ouahigouya *Burkina Faso* 42C3
Ouargla *Algeria* 42D1
Oudtshoorn *South Africa* 44C4
Oujda *Morocco* 42C1
Oulu *Finland* 30F2
Outer Hebrides *Scotland* 22A3
Oviedo *Spain* 25A1
Oxford *England* 21F6
Oyem *Gabon* 42E4

P

Padang *Indonesia* 36C4
Paderborn *Germany* 28B2
Pag I. *Croatia* 26D2
Pagai Selatan I. *Indonesia* 36C4
Pagai Utara I. *Indonesia* 36B4
Pahala *Hawaii USA* 6H
Paisley *Scotland* 22D5
Pais Vasco *Region Spain* 25B1
Pakistan 39F2
Palangkaraya *Indonesia* 36D4
Palau Is. *see* Belau 37F3
Palawan I. *Philippines* 36D2
Palembang *Indonesia* 36C4
Palencia *Spain* 25B1
Palermo *Italy* 26C3
Palma de Mallorca *Spain* 25C2
Palmerston North *New Zealand* 45G5
Palmi *Italy* 26D3
Palmyra *Pacific Ocean* 47
Palu *Indonesia* 36D4
Pamplona *Spain* 25B1
Panamá *Panama* 14D5
Panay I. *Philippines* 37E2
Pangkalpinang *Indonesia* 36C4
Pantelleria I. *Italy* 26C3
Papa Westray I. *Scotland* 22F1
Papua New Guinea 37G4
Pará *State Brazil* 16D3
Paracel Is. *South China Sea* 36D2
Paracin *Yugoslavia* 27E2
Paraíba *State Brazil* 16F3
Parakou *Benin* 42D4
Paramaribo *Suriname* 16D2
Paraná *Argentina* 17C6
Parana *State Brazil* 17D5
Paraguay 17D5
Parepare *Indonesia* 36D4
Paris *France* 24C2
Parkano *Finland* 30E3
Parma *Italy* 26C2
Parnaíba *Brazil* 16E3
Pärnu *Estonia* 30E4
Pasadena *USA* 6B2
Passo Fundo *Brazil* 17D5
Pasto *Colombia* 16B2
Patna *India* 39G3
Pátrai *Greece* 27E3
Pau *France* 24B3
Pavlodar *Kazakhstan* 32J4
P. Dolak I. *Indonesia* 37F4
Pec *Serbia* 27E2
Pécs *Hungary* 29D3
Peebles *Scotland* 22E5
Pegu *Myanmar* 36B2
Pekanbaru *Indonesia* 36C3
Peking *see* Beijing 35F3
Pello *Finland* 30E2
Pelopónnisos (Peloponnese) *Greece* 27E3
Pemba I. *Tanzania* 43G5
Pemba *Mozambique* 44E2
Pembroke *Wales* 21C6
Pennsylvania *State USA* 7F1
Penrith *England* 20E3
Penza *Russia* 32F4
Penzance *England* 20B7
Pereira *Colombia* 16B2
Périgueux *France* 24C2
Perm *Russia* 32G4
Pernambuco *State Brazil* 16F3
Perpignan *France* 24C3
Perth *Australia* 45A4
Perth *Scotland* 22E4
Peru 16B4
Perugia *Italy* 26C2
Pescara *Italy* 26C2
Peshawar *Pakistan* 39F2
Peterborough *England* 21G5
Peterhead *Scotland* 22G3
Petropavlovsk Kamchatskiy *Russia* 33R4
Petropavlovsk *Kazakhstan* 32H4
Petrozavodsk *Russia* 32E3
Philadelphia *USA* 7F1
Philippines 37E2
Phitsanulok *Thailand* 36C2
Phnom Penh *Cambodia* 36C2
Phoenix Is. *Kiribati* 46
Phoenix *USA* 6B2
Phuket I. *Thailand* 36B3
Pila *Poland* 28D2
Piacenza *Italy* 26B1
Piauí *State Brazil* 16E3
Picardie (Picardy) *Province France* 24C2
Pierre *USA* 6C1
Pietermaritzburg *South Africa* 44D3
Pietersburg *South Africa* 44C3
Pílos *Greece* 27E3
Pinar del Rio *Cuba* 14C2
Pingliang *China* 34E3
Piombino *Italy* 26C2
Piraiévs *Greece* 27E3
Pírgos *Greece* 27E3
Pirot *Yugoslavia* 27E2
Pisa *Italy* 26C2
Pitcairn I. *Pacific Ocean* 47
Piteå *Sweden* 30E2
Pitesti *Romania* 27E2
Pitlochry *Scotland* 22E4
Pittsburgh *USA* 7F1
Piura *Peru* 16A3
Plasencia *Spain* 25A1
Pleven *Bulgaria* 27E2
Ploiesti *Romania* 27F2
Plovdiv *Bulgaria* 27E2
Plymouth *England* 21C7
Plzen *Czech Republic* 28C3
Pointe-á-Pitre *Guadeloupe* 14G3
Pointe Noire *Congo* 42E5
Poitiers *France* 24C2
Poitou *Province France* 24B2
Poland 29D2
Polla *Italy* 26D2
Poltava *Ukraine* 32E5
Ponce *Puerto Rico* 14F3
Ponferrada *Spain* 25A1
Pontevedra *Spain* 25A1
Pontianak *Indonesia* 36C4
Poole *England* 21F7
Pori *Finland* 30E3
Port Augusta *Australia* 45C4
Port au Prince *Haiti* 14E3
Port Elizabeth *South Africa* 44C4
Port Gentil *Gabon* 42D5
Port Harcourt *Nigeria* 42D4
Port Headland *Australia* 45A3
Portland *USA* 6A1
Port Laoise *Ireland* 23D3
Port Louis *Mauritius* 44F4
Port Moresby *Papua New Guinea* 37G4
Porto *Portugal* 25A1
Pôrto Alegre *Brazil* 17D6
Port of Spain *Trinidad* 14G4
Porto Novo *Benin* 42D3/4
Porto Torres *Italy* 26B2
Porto Vecchio *France* 26B2
Pôrto Velho *Brazil* 16C3
Port Pirie *Australia* 45C4
Portrush *Northern Ireland* 23E1
Port Said *Egypt* 43G1
Portsmouth *England* 21F7
Port Sudan *Sudan* 43G3
Port Talbot *Wales* 21D6
Portugal 25A1/2
Poso *Indonesia* 37E4
Potchefstroom *South Africa* 44C3
Potenza *Italy* 26D2
Potosí *Bolivia* 16C4
Potsdam *Germany* 28C2
Poznan *Poland* 28D2
Praha (Prague) *Czech Republic* 28C2
Prato *Italy* 26C2
Preston *England* 20E4
Preswick *Scotland* 22D5
Pretoria *South Africa* 44C3
Prince Edward I. *Canada* 5M5
Prince George *Canada* 5F4
Prince of Wales I. *Canada* 5H/J2
Prince Rupert *Canada* 5F4
Príncipe I. *W. Africa* 42D4
Pristina *Yugoslavia* 27E2
Prokop'yevsk *Russia* 32K4
Prome *Myanmar* 36B2
Provence *Province France* 24D3
Providence *USA* 7F1
Prudhoe Bay *USA* 6J
Przemys'l *Poland* 29E3
Pskov *Russia* 32D4
Pucallpa *Peru* 16B3
Puebla *Mexico* 6D4
Puerto Armuelles *Panama* 14C5
Puerto Ayacucho *Venezuela* 16C2
Puerto Barrios *Guatemala* 14B3
Puerto Cabezas *Nicaragua* 14C4
Puerto Cortés *Honduras* 14B3
Puerto Juárez *Mexico* 7E3
Puertollano *Spain* 25B2
Puerto Montt *Chile* 17B7
Puerto Plata *Dominican Republic* 14E3
Puerto Rico I. *Caribbean Sea* 14F3
Pula *Croatia* 26C2
Pune *India* 39F4
Punta Arenas *Chile* 16B8
Puntarenas *Costa Rica* 14C5
Pusan *South Korea* 35G3
Puttgarden *Germany* 28C2
Pyongyang *China* 35G3

Q

Qamdo *China* 34D3
Qatar 38D3
Qazvin *Iran* 38C2
Qena *Egypt* 43G2
Qingdao *China* 35G3
Qinghai *Province China* 34D3
Qingjiang *China* 35F3
Qinhuangdao *China* 35F2
Qiqihar *China* 35G2
Qom *Iran* 38D2
Quanzhou *China* 35F4
Québec *Canada* 5L5
Québec *Province Canada* 5L4/5
Queen Charlotte Is. *Canada* 5E4
Queen Elizabeth Is. *Canada* 5G2
Queensland *State Australia* 45D3
Quelimane *Mozambique* 44D2
Quetta *Pakistan* 39E3
Quezaltenango *Guatemala* 14A4
Quezon City *Philippines* 37E2
Qui Nhon *Vietnam* 36C2
Quilon *India* 39F5
Quimper *France* 24B2
Quito *Ecuador* 16B3
Qu Xian *China* 35F4

R

Raasay I. *Scotland* 22B3
Rab I. *Croatia* 26C2
Raba *Indonesia* 36D4
Rabat *Morocco* 42C1
Radom *Poland* 29E2
Raipur *India* 39G3
Rajkot *India* 39F3
Raleigh *USA* 7F2
Ramsey *Isle of Man* 20C3
Rancagua *Chile* 17B6
Ranchi *India* 39G3
Randers *Denmark* 30C4
Rangoon *see* Yangon 36B2
Rangpur *Bangladesh* 39G3
Rapid City *USA* 6C1
Rasht *Iran* 38C2
Rathlin I. *Northern Ireland* 23E1
Ráth Luirc *Ireland* 23C4
Ratlam *India* 39F3
Rauma *Finland* 30E3
Ravenna *Italy* 26C2
Rawalpindi *Pakistan* 39F2
Razgrad *Bulgaria* 27F2
Reading *England* 21G6
Recife *Brazil* 16F3
Redon *France* 24B2
Regensburg *Germany* 28C3
Reggane *Algeria* 42D2
Reggio di Calabria *Italy* 26D3
Reggio nell'Emilia *Italy* 26C2
Regina *Canada* 5H4
Reims *France* 24C2
Renell I. *Solomon Islands* 45F2
Rennes *France* 24B2
Reno *USA* 6B2
Resistencia *Argentina* 17D5
Resolution I. *Canada* 5M3
Réunion I. *Indian Ocean* 44F4
Reykjavík *Iceland* 30A2
Rhode Island *State USA* 7F1
Rhodes I. *see* Ródhos 27F3
Rhum I. *Scotland* 22B3/4
Rhyl *Wales* 20D4
Richmond *USA* 7F2
Riga *Latvia* 32D4
Rijeka *Croatia* 26C1
Rimini *Italy* 26C2
Rîmnicu Vîlcea *Romania* 29E3
Ringwood *England* 21F7
Rio Branco *Brazil* 16C3
Rio de Janeiro *Brazil* 16E5
Rio de Janeiro *State Brazil* 16E5
Río Gallegos *Argentina* 16C8
Rio Grande do Norte *State Brazil* 16F3
Rio Grande do Sul *State Brazil* 17D5/6
Rio Grande *Brazil* 17D6
Río Negro *State Argentina* 17C7
Ripon *England* 20F3
Riyadh *see* Ar Riyad 38C3
Roanne *France* 24C2
Rochdale *England* 20E4
Rochester *England* 21H6
Rochester *USA* 7D1
Rockford *USA* 7E1
Rockhampton *Australia* 45E3
Rødbyhavn *Denmark* 30C5
Ródhos (Rhodes) *Greece* 27F3
Roma (Rome) *Italy* 26C2
Roman *Romania* 29F3
Romania 27E/F1
Rome *see* Roma 26C2
Ronda *Spain* 25A2
Rondônia *State Brazil* 16C4
Rosario *Argentina* 17C6
Roscoff *France* 24B2

Roscommon *Ireland* 23C3
Roscrea *Ireland* 23D4
Roseau *Dominica* 14G3
Rosslare *Ireland* 23E4
Rostock *Germany* 28C2
Rostov-na-Donu *Russia* 32E5
Rotherham *England* 20F4
Roti I. *Indonesia* 37E5
Rotterdam *Netherlands* 28A2
Rouen *France* 24C2
Round I. *Mauritius* 44F4
Rousay I. *Scotland* 22E1
Roussillon *Province France* 24C3
Rovaniemi *Finland* 30F2
Royal Tunbridge Wells *England* 21H6
Ruffec *France* 24C2
Rugby *England* 21F5
Rügen I. *Germany* 28C2
Ruma *Yugoslavia* 27D1
Runcorn *England* 20E4
Ruoqiang *China* 34C3
Ruse *Bulgaria* 27F2
Russian Federation 32/33
Ruteng *Indonesia* 37E4
Rwanda 43G5
Ryazan' *Russia* 32E4
Rybinsk *Russia* 32E4
Rybnik *Poland* 29D2
Ryukyu Is. *Japan* 35G4
Rzeszów *Poland* 29E2

S

Saarbrücken *Germany* 28B3
Saaremaa I. *Estonia* 30E4
Sabac *Yugoslavia* 27D2
Sabadell *Spain* 25C1
Sabha *Libya* 42E2
Sacramento *USA* 6A2
Sadiya *India* 39H3
Safi *Morocco* 42C1
Sagunto *Spain* 25B2
Saintes *France* 24B2
Sakai *Japan* 35L9
Sakata *Japan* 35N7
Sakhalin I. *Russia* 33Q4
Sakishima gunto I. *Japan* 34G4
Salalah *Oman* 38D4
Salamanca *Spain* 25A1
Salangen *Norway* 30D2
Salayar I. *Indonesia* 37E4
Salbris *France* 24C2
Salem *India* 39F4
Salem *USA* 6A1
Salerno *Italy* 26C2
Salford *England* 20E4
Salisbury *England* 21F6
Salo *Finland* 30E3
Salonta *Romania* 29E3
Salta *Argentina* 16C5
Salta *State Argentina* 16C5
Saltillo *Mexico* 6C3
Salt Lake City *USA* 6B1
Salto *Uruguay* 17D6
Salvador *Brazil* 16F4
Salzburg *Austria* 28C3
Salzgitter-Bad *Germany* 28C2
Samara *Russia* 32G4
Samar I. *Philippines* 37E2
Samarinda *Indonesia* 36D4
Samarkand *Uzbekistan* 32H6
Samoa *Pacific Ocean* 46
Sámos I. *Greece* 27F3
Samothráki I. *Greece* 27F2
Samsun *Turkey* 38B1
San *Mali* 42C3
San'a *Yemen* 38C4
San Antonio *USA* 6D3
San Benedetto del Tronto *Italy* 26C2
San Cristobal I. *Solomon Islands* 45F2
San Cristóbal *Venezuela* 16B2
Sancti Spíritus *Cuba* 14D2
Sandakan *Malaysia.* 36D3
Sanday I. *Scotland* 22F1
San Diego *USA* 6B2
Sandoy I. *Denmark* 30A2
San Fernando *Philippines* 37E2
San Francisco *USA* 6A2
Sanjo *Japan* 35N8
San José *Costa Rica* 14C5
San Jose *USA* 6A2
San Juan *Argentina* 17C6
San Juan *Puerto Rico* 14F3
San Juan del Norte *Nicaragua* 14C4
San Juan del Sur *Nicaragua* 14B4
San Juan *State Argentina* 17C6
San Julián *Argentina* 17C7
Sankt Peterburg (St Petersburg) *Russia* 32E4
San Luis Potosí *Mexico* 6C3
San Luis *State Argentina* 17C6
San Marino *San Marino* 26C2
Sanmenxia *China* 35F3
San Miguel *El Salvador* 14B4
San Miguel de Tucumán *Argentina* 16C5
San Pedro Sula *Honduras* 14B3
San Remo *Italy* 26B2
San Salvador *El Salvador* 14B4
San Salvador I. *The Bahamas* 14D/E1
San Sebastian *Spain* 25B1
San Severo *Italy* 26D2
Santa Ana *El Salvador* 14B4
Santa Catarina *State Brazil* 17D5
Santa Clara *Cuba* 14C2
Santa Cruz Is. *Solomon Islands* 45F2
Santa Cruz *Bolivia* 16C4
Santa Cruz *State Argentina* 17B/C7
Santa Fe *USA* 6C2
Santa Fé *Argentina* 17C6
Santa Fé *State Argentina* 17C5/6
Santa Isabel I. *Solomon Islands* 45E1
Santa Marta *Colombia* 16B1
Santander *Spain* 25B1
Santarém *Brazil* 16D3
Santarém *Portugal* 25A2
Santa Rosa *Argentina* 17C6
Santiago *Chile* 17B6
Santiago *Dominican Republic* 14E3
Santiago *Panama* 14C5
Santiago de Compostela *Spain* 25A1
Santiago de Cuba *Cuba* 14D3
Santiago del Estero *State Argentina* 16C5
Santo Domingo *Dominican Republic* 14F3
São Carlos *Brazil* 16E5
São Luis *Brazil* 16E3
São Paulo *Brazil* 16E5
São Paulo *State Brazil* 16E5
São Tomé I. *W. Africa* 42D4
São Tomé and Príncipe Rep. *W. Africa* 42D4
Sapporo *Japan* 35J2
Sapri *Italy* 26D2
Sarajevo *Bosnia* 27D2
Saratov *Russia* 32F4
Sardegna I. (Sardinia) *Italy* 26B2/3
Sardinia *see* Sardegna 26B2
Sarh *Chad* 43E4
Sark I. *UK* 21E8
Sarrion *Spain* 25B1
Sasebo *Japan* 35G3
Saskatchewan *Province Canada* 5H4
Saskatoon *Canada* 5H4
Sassandra *Côte d'Ivoire* 42C4
Sassari *Sardegna* 26B2
Sassnitz *Germany* 28C2
Satu Mare *Romania* 29E3
Saudi Arabia 38C3
Saul Ste Marie *Canada* 5K5
Savannah *USA* 7E2
Savannakhet *Laos* 36C2
Savoie (Savoy) *Province France* 24D2
Savona *Italy* 26B2
Savonlinna *Finland* 30F3
Savoy *see* Savoie 24D2
Saxmundham *England* 21J5
Saynshand *Mongolia* 35F2
Scarborough *England* 20G3
Schwerin *Germany* 28C2
Scilly Isles *see* Isles of Scilly 21A8
Scourie *Scotland* 22C2
Scunthorpe *England* 20G4
Seattle *USA* 6A1
Seaward Pen. *USA* 5B3
Sebes *Romania* 29E3
Ségou *Mali* 42C3
Segovia Spain 25B1
Seinäjoki *Finland* 30E3
Sekondi *Ghana* 42C4
Selby *England* 20F4
Semarang *Indonesia* 36D4
Semipalatinsk *Kazakhstan* 32K4
Sendai *Japan* 35P7
Senegal 42B3
Senlis *France* 24C2
Sennen *England* 20D7
Sens *France* 24C2
Seoul *see* Soul 35G3
Seram I. *Indonesia* 37E4
Serbia Republic 27E2
Sergino *Russia* 32H3
Sergipe *State Brazil* 16F4
Sérifos *Greece* 27E3
Serov *Russia* 32H4
Serpukhov *Russia* 32E4
Sérrai *Greece* 27E2
Sétif *Algeria* 42D1
Setúbal *Portugal* 25A2
Sevastopol' *Ukraine* 32E5
Severnaya Zemlya *Russia* 33L2
Severodvinsk *Russia* 32E3
Sevilla *Spain* 25A2
Seychelles Is. *Indian Ocean* 44F1
Seydhisfödhur *Iceland* 30C1
Sézanne *France* 24C2
Sfax *Tunisia* 42E1
's-Gravenhage *Netherlands* 28A2
Shado shima I. *Japan* 35N7
Shahjahanpur *India* 39G3
Shakhty *Russia* 32F5
Shandong *Province China* 35F3
Shanghai *China* 35G3
Shangrao *China* 35F4
Shantou *China* 35F4
Shanxi *Province China* 35F3
Shaoguan *China* 35F4
Shaoxing *China* 35G4
Shaoyang *China* 35F4
Shapinsay I. *Scotland* 22F1
Shashi *China* 35F3
Sheffield *England* 20F4
Shenyang *China* 35G2
Shetland Is. *Scotland* 22J7
Shijiazhuang *China* 35F3
Shillong *India* 39H3
Shimizu *Japan* 35N9
Shingu *Japan* 35L10
Shíraz *Iran* 38D3
Shizuoka *Japan* 35N9
Shkodër *Albania* 27D2
Shreveport *USA* 7D2
Shrewsbury *England* 21E5
Shuangyashan *China* 35H2
Sialkot *Pakistan* 39F2
Siauliai *Lithuania* 30E5
Sibenik *Croatia* 26D2
Siberut I. *Indonesia* 36B4
Sibiu *Romania* 29E3
Sibolga *Indonesia* 36B3
Sibu *Malaysia* 36D3
Sichuan *Province China* 34E3
Sidi Bel Abbès *Algeria* 42C1
Siedlce *Poland* 29E2
Siegen *Germany* 28B2
Siena *Italy* 26C2
Sierra Leone 42B4
Sifnos I. *Greece* 27E3
Sigüenza *Spain* 25B1
Siguiri *Guinea* 42C3
Sikasso *Mali* 42C3
Síkinos I. *Greece* 27E3
Simeulue I. *Indonesia* 36B4
Singapore 36C3
Singkawang *Indonesia* 36C3
Sintra *Portugal* 25A2
Sioux Falls *USA* 6D1
Siping *China* 35G2
Sipora I. *Indonesia* 36B4
Siracusa *Italy* 26D3
Síros I. *Greece* 27E3
Sisak *Croatia* 26D1
Sittwe *Myanmar* 36B1
Sivas *Turkey* 38B2
Sjaelland I. *Denmark* 30C4
Skara *Sweden* 30C4
Skegness *England* 20H4
Skellefteå *Sweden* 30E3
Skíathos I. *Greece* 27E3
Skien *Norway* 30B4
Skikda *Algeria* 42D1
Skiros *Greece* 27E3
Skópelos I. *Greece* 27E3
Skopje *Macedonia* 27E2
Skovorodino *Russia* 33O4
Skye I. *Scotland* 22B3
Slatina *Romania* 27E2
Sligo *Ireland* 23C2
Slovakia 29D/E3
Sliven *Bulgaria* 27F2
Smolensk *Russia* 32E4
Sobral *Brazil* 16E3
Société Is. 47
Socotra I. *Yemen* 38D4
Sodankylä *Finland* 30F2
Söderhamn *Sweden* 30D3
Södertälje *Sweden* 30D4
Sofiya (Sofia) *Bulgaria* 27E2
Sokodé *Togo* 42D4
Sokoto *Nigeria* 42D3
Solapur *India* 39F4
Sollefteå *Sweden* 30D3
Solomon Is. *Pacific Ocean* 45F1/2
Somalia 43H4
Somerset I. *Canada* 5J2
Sondrio *Italy* 26B1
Songkhla *Thailand* 36C3
Sorocaba *Brazil* 16E5
Sorong *Indonesia* 37F4
Soroti *Uganda* 43G4
Sorrento *Italy* 26C2
Sorsele *Sweden* 30D2
Sosnowiec *Poland* 29D2
Souillac *France* 24C3
Soul (Seoul) *South Korea* 35G3
South Africa *Republic of* 44C4
Southampton *England* 21F7
Southampton I. *Canada* 5K3
South Australia *State Australia* 45C3/4
South Carolina *State USA* 7E2
South Dakota *State USA* 6C/D1
Southend-on-Sea *England* 21H6
South Georgia I. *South Atlantic Ocean* 17F8
South Island *New Zealand* 45F/G5
Southport *England* 20D4
South Ronaldsay I. *Scotland* 22F2
South Shields *England* 20F3
South Uist I. *Scotland* 22A3
Sovetskaya Gavan' *Russia* 33Q5
Soweto *South Africa* 44C3
Spain 25
Spalding *England* 21G5
Spitsbergen *see* Svalbard 32C2
Split *Croatia* 26D2
Spokane *USA* 6B1
Spratly Islands *South China Sea* 36D2
Springfield *Missouri USA* 7D2
Springfield *Illinois USA* 7E2
Springs *South Africa* 44C3
Sri Lanka 39G5
Srinagar *India* 39F2
Sta Cruz de Tenerife *Canary Islands* 42B2
Stafford *England* 20E5
St Albans *England* 21G6
St Andrews *Scotland* 22F4
Stanley *Falkland Islands* 17D8
Stara Zagora *Bulgaria* 27F2
Starbuck I. *Kiribati* 47
St Austell *England* 21C7
Stavanger *Norway* 30B4
Stavropol' *Russia* 32F5
St Brieuc *France* 24B2
St Croix I. *Caribbean Sea* 14G3
St David's *Wales* 20B6
St Denis *Réunion* 44F4
St Dizier *France* 24C2
Steinkjer *Norway* 30C3
St Étienne *France* 24C2
Stewart I. *New Zealand* 45F5
St Gaudens *France* 24C3
St George's *Grenada* 14G4
St Helens *England* 20E4
St Helier *Jersey* 21E8
Stirling *Scotland* 22E4
St Ives *England* 21B7
St John's *Antigua* 14G3
St John's *Canada* 5N5
St John *Canada* 5M5
St Kitts Is. *Caribbean* 14G3
St Lawrence I. *USA* 6J
St Lawrence I. *USA* 5A3/33U3
St Louis *Senegal* 42B3
St Louis *USA* 7D2
St Lucia I. *Caribbean* 14G4
St Malo *France* 24B2
St Martin *Caribbean Sea* 14G3
St Martin's I. *England* 20A8
St Mary's I. *England* 20A8
St Nazaire *France* 24B2
Stockport *England* 20E4
Stoke-on-Trent *England* 20E4
Stonehaven *Scotland* 22F4
Stören *Norway* 30C3
Storlien *Sweden* 30C3
Stornoway *Scotland* 22B2
Storuman *Sweden* 30D2
St Paul *USA* 7D1
St Peter Port *Guernsey* 21E8
St Petersburg *see* Sankt Peterburg 32E4
St Petersburg *USA* 7E3
St Quentin *France* 24C2
Strabane *Northern Ireland* 23D2
Stralsund *Germany* 28C2
Stranraer *Scotland* 22D6
Strasbourg *France* 24D2
Stratford-on-Avon *England* 21F5
Streymoy I. *Denmark* 30A2
Strömsund *Sweden* 30D3
Stronsay I. *Scotland* 22F1
Stroud *England* 21E6
St Tropez *France* 24D3
Stuttgart *Germany* 28B3
St Vincent I. *Caribbean* 14G4
Subotica *Yugoslavia* 27D1
Suceava *Romania* 29F3
Sucre *Bolivia* 16C4
Sudan 43F/G3
Suduroy I. *Denmark* 30A2
Suez *Egypt* 43G2
Sukhumi *Georgia* 32F5
Sukkur *Pakistan* 39E3
Sulawesi *Indonesia* 37E4
Sulu Arch. *Philippines* 37E3
Sumba I. *Indonesia* 36D4
Sumbawa I. *Indonesia* 36D4
Sumen *Bulgaria* 27F2
Sumy *Ukraine* 32E4
Sunderland *England* 20F3
Sundsvall *Sweden* 30D3
Suntar *Russia* 33N3
Surabaya *Indonesia* 36D4
Surakarta *Indonesia* 36D4
Surat *India* 39F3
Surgut *Russia* 32J3
Suriname 16D2
Surtsey I. *Iceland* 30A2
Suva *Fiji* 46
Suzhou *China* 35G3
Svalbard Is. *Norway* 32C2
Sveg *Sweden* 30C3
Sverdrup Is. *Canada* 5H2
Svetozarevo *Yugoslavia* 27E2
Swakopmund *South Africa* 44B3
Swan I. *Honduras* 14C3
Swansea *Wales* 21D6
Swaziland Kingdom *South Africa* 44D3
Sweden 30
Swindon *England* 21F6
Switzerland 28B3
Sydney *Australia* 45E4
Syktyvkar *Russia* 32G3
Syracuse *USA* 7F1
Syzran' *Russia* 32F4
Szczecin *Poland* 28C2
Szczecinek *Poland* 28D2
Szeged *Hungary* 29E3
Székesfehérvár *Hungary* 29D3
Szekszárd *Hungary* 29D3
Szolnok *Hungary* 29E3

T

Tabora *Tanzania* 43G5
Tabriz *Iran* 38C2
Tabuaeran I. *Kiribati* 46
Tabuk *Saudi Arabia* 38B3
Taegu *South Korea* 35G3
Taejon *South Korea* 35G3
Tahiti I. *Pacific Ocean* 47
Tahoua *Niger* 42D3
Tái-nan *Taiwan* 37E1
T'ai-pei *Taiwan* 37E1
Taiwan Republic *China* 37E1
Taiyuan *China* 35F3
Ta'izz *Yemen* 38C4
Tajikistan 32H/J6
Takada *Japan* 35N8
Takaoka *Japan* 35M8
Takasaki *Japan* 35N8
Takoradi *Ghana* 42C4
Talavera de la Reina *Spain* 25B2
Talca *Chile* 17B6
Talcahuano *Chile* 17B6
Tallahassee *USA* 7E2
Tallinn *Estonia* 32D4
Tamale *Ghana* 42C4
Tamanrasset *Algeria* 42D2
Tambacounda *Senegal* 42B3
Tampa *USA* 7E3
Tampere *Finland* 30E3
Tampico *Mexico* 6D3
Tamworth *Australia* 45E4
Tanga *Tanzania* 43G5
Tanger *Morocco* 42C1
Tangshan *China* 35F3
Tanna I. *Vanuatu* 45F2
Tanta *Egypt* 43G1
Tanzania 43G5
Taolanaro *Madagascar* 44E3
Tarabulus (Tripoli) *Libya* 42E1
Tarakan I. *Indonesia/Malaysia* 36D3
Tarancón *Spain* 25B1
Taranto *Italy* 27D2
Tarbert *Ireland* 23B4
Tarbert *Strathclyde Scotland* 22C5
Tarbert *Western Isles Scotland* 22B3
Tarbes *France* 24C3
Tarcoola *Australia* 45C4
Tarfaya *Morocco* 42B2
Tarnów *Poland* 29E2
Tarragona *Spain* 25C1
Tarrasa *Spain* 25C1
Tarutung *Indonesia* 36B3
Tashkent *Uzbekistan* 32H5
Taunton *England* 21D6
Tavira *Portugal* 25A2
Tavoy *Myanmar* 36B2
Tawau *Malaysia* 36D3
Tawitawi *Philippines* 37E3
Tbilisi *Georgia* 32F5
Tecuci *Romania* 29F3
Tegucigalpa *Honduras* 14B4
Tehran *Iran* 38D2
Tehuantepec *Mexico* 7D4
Tel Aviv *Israel* 38B2
Telford *England* 21E5
Telukbetung *Indonesia* 36C4
Temuco *Chile* 17B6
Tenerife *Canary Islands* 42B2
Tennant Creek *Australia* 45C2
Tennessee *State USA* 7E2
Teófilo Otôni *Brazil* 16E4
Teresina *Brazil* 16E3
Termez *Uzbekistan* 32H6
Termoli *Italy* 26C2
Terni *Italy* 26C2